COMPACT *Research*

Methamphetamine

Drugs

ReferencePoint
Press®

San Diego, CA

Other books in the Compact Research Drugs set:

*For a complete list of titles please visit www.referencepointpress.com.

COMPACT *Research*

Methamphetamine

Peggy J. Parks

Drugs

ReferencePoint
Press®

San Diego, CA

© 2014 ReferencePoint Press, Inc.
Printed in the United States

For more information, contact:
ReferencePoint Press, Inc.
PO Box 27779
San Diego, CA 92198
www.ReferencePointPress.com

Picture credits:
Cover: iStockphoto.com
AP Images: 18
© Bart Ah You/Zuma Press/Corbis: 16
Steve Zmina: 33–35, 47–48, 61–63, 75–77

LIBRARY OF CONGRESS CATALOGING-IN-PUBLICATION DATA

Parks, Peggy J., 1951–
    Methamphetamine / by Peggy J. Parks.
        pages cm. -- (Compact research series)
    Includes bibliographical references and index.
    Audience: Grade 9 to 12.
    ISBN-13: 978-1-60152-520-8 (hardback)
    ISBN-10: 1-60152-520-6 (hardback)
 1. Methamphetamine abuse--Juvenile literature. I. Title.
    RC568.A45P37   2014
    362.29'95--dc23
                                                    2013009272

Contents

Foreword

As modern civilization continues to evolve, its ability to create, store, distribute, and access information expands exponentially. The explosion of information from all media continues to increase at a phenomenal rate. By 2020 some experts predict the worldwide information base will double every seventy-three days. While access to diverse sources of information and perspectives is paramount to any democratic society, information alone cannot help people gain knowledge and understanding. Information must be organized and presented clearly and succinctly in order to be understood. The challenge in the digital age becomes not the creation of information, but how best to sort, organize, enhance, and present information.

ReferencePoint Press developed the *Compact Research* series with this challenge of the information age in mind. More than any other subject area today, researching current issues can yield vast, diverse, and unqualified information that can be intimidating and overwhelming for even the most advanced and motivated researcher. The *Compact Research* series offers a compact, relevant, intelligent, and conveniently organized collection of information covering a variety of current topics ranging from illegal immigration and deforestation to diseases such as anorexia and meningitis.

The series focuses on three types of information: objective single-author narratives, opinion-based primary source quotations, and facts and statistics. The clearly written objective narratives provide context and reliable background information. Primary source quotes are carefully selected and cited, exposing the reader to differing points of view, and facts and statistics sections aid the reader in evaluating perspectives. Presenting these key types of information creates a richer, more balanced learning experience.

For better understanding and convenience, the series enhances information by organizing it into narrower topics and adding design features that make it easy for a reader to identify desired content. For example, in *Compact Research: Illegal Immigration*, a chapter covering the economic impact of illegal immigration has an objective narrative explaining the various ways the economy is impacted, a balanced section of numerous primary source quotes on the topic, followed by facts and full-color illustrations to encourage evaluation of contrasting perspectives.

The ancient Roman philosopher Lucius Annaeus Seneca wrote, "It is quality rather than quantity that matters." More than just a collection of content, the *Compact Research* series is simply committed to creating, finding, organizing, and presenting the most relevant and appropriate amount of information on a current topic in a user-friendly style that invites, intrigues, and fosters understanding.

Methamphetamine at a Glance

Characteristics of Methamphetamine

Methamphetamine is a powerful and addictive stimulant drug that may be either powder or rock; depending on its form, meth may be smoked, snorted, dissolved in liquid and drunk, or injected.

Legal Uses

Methamphetamine is classified as a Schedule II controlled substance, so it can legally be prescribed by a doctor for several medical conditions.

Warning Signs of Meth Abuse

Methamphetamine abusers are often hyperactive and jittery, lose interest in food (leading to weight loss), have skin that is peppered with open sores, have bad teeth and gums, and age prematurely.

Meth Making

Methamphetamine can be made almost anywhere, from enormous superlabs to the backseat of a car using the shake-and-bake method.

Seriousness of Problem

A November 2012 report showed that 439,000 people in the United States aged twelve and older were current meth users in 2011, which is an increase over 2010.

Dangers of Meth Abuse

Habitual meth use is extremely risky and can cause everything from skin infections and loss of teeth to stroke, heart disease, and cancer.

Effects of Laws

The 2005 Combat Methamphetamine Epidemic Act made a significant improvement in cutting meth lab incidents in the United States, but its success was short-lived. As a result, states are passing their own legislation in an effort to fight the problem.

Treatment

Meth addiction is known for being extremely difficult to treat and has a high relapse rate, although people can and do recover after treatment.

Prevention

Drug experts say the key to meth abuse prevention is education programs that dissuade people from ever trying the drug.

Overview

By the time Nic Sheff was eighteen years old he had used just about every kind of street drug. Two drugs that he had not tried were heroin (because he was afraid of it) and methamphetamine (because he knew nothing about it). "I'm not sure if I was living in a bubble or what," says Sheff, "but I'd never even really heard of meth before I first tried it." That changed one night when his friend suggested they go to a nearby town to get some "speed," and Sheff was introduced to a potent, crystalline form of methamphetamine known as crystal meth. He and his friend crushed it into powder and snorted it through a cut plastic straw, and Sheff was stunned at how fast and powerful its effects were. "Instantly," he says, "right when the drug hit me, it was the most incredible feeling I'd ever known in my whole life."[1]

Sheff soon learned that the "incredible feeling" was short-lived. It was followed by an overpowering urge for more methamphetamine, which led to an addiction that dominated his life for five years. He writes: "Nothing could have prepared me [for] how genuinely life altering and world shattering that first line of speed would be for me." Today, Sheff talks freely about his experience as a meth addict and has written two books about his horrific battle with the drug that he now refers to as "nasty," "sinister," "dirty," and "disgusting." "It just deserves to be wiped off the face of the earth," he says. "It destroyed my life. And it's destroyed so many people's lives. There is truly nothing redeeming about it."[2]

What Is Methamphetamine?

Methamphetamine is in a class of drugs known as stimulants, which are so named because they stimulate, or excite, the central nervous system. Meth is a synthetic drug, meaning one that is created (synthesized) entirely from human-made chemicals rather than natural substances. This distinguishes it from plant-derived drugs such as heroin, which is produced from opium poppies, and cocaine, which is made from leaves of the coca plant.

Meth is similar in structure to amphetamines, which are also stimulants. But these drugs are not exactly the same, as the National Institute on Drug Abuse (NIDA) explains: "Like amphetamine, methamphetamine causes increased activity and talkativeness, decreased appetite, and a general sense of well-being. However, methamphetamine differs from amphetamine in that at comparable doses, much higher levels of methamphetamine get into the brain, making it a more potent stimulant drug."[3]

Street methamphetamine is typically found in two forms: powder and rock. Powder meth is odorless, bitter-tasting, and usually white or a brownish color. In addition to "meth" and "speed" it is referred to by slang terms such as "tweak," "chalk," "crank," and "redneck cocaine." The powder may be inhaled through the nose (snorted), sprinkled on food and

> " Even though methamphetamine is a synthetic drug, its roots trace back to ancient times and an evergreen shrub known as ephedra. "

eaten, dissolved in liquid and drunk, heated in a spoon and injected into a vein, or smoked in a pipe. Crystal meth, the rock form of the drug, may also be smoked as well as crushed and snorted or heated and injected in a vein. It is clear or has a bluish tinge, looks like chunky crystals or glass shards, and is often referred to by street names such as crystal, ice, glass, crissy, tina, and blade.

Roots in Ancient Medicine

Even though methamphetamine is a synthetic drug, its roots trace back to ancient times and an evergreen shrub known as ephedra. The shrub still grows wild in China and certain other areas of the world, and was used for medicinal purposes as far back as 3000 BC. Tea made with ephedra (ma huang in Chinese) was found to widen the major air passages in the lungs, so it was used to treat asthma and other breathing problems, as well as nasal congestion. In the late nineteenth century ephedra's main active ingredient, ephedrine, was identified and extracted by Japanese chemist Nagayoshi Nagai.

In 1893 Nagai became the first to synthesize methamphetamine, although his accomplishment did not attract much attention. A key turning point was in 1919 when another Japanese chemist, Akira Ogata, created a crystallized version of the drug. Awareness of meth as a powerful stimulant grew during the 1920s and 1930s, and in some parts of the world its use grew rapidly. During World War II meth was freely distributed to German and Japanese soldiers to help stave off fatigue, increase concentration, and boost energy levels. Japanese suicide pilots (known as kamikazes) were given meth to prepare them for missions in which they were going to die, as a Japanese man named Koichi writes: "Kamikaze pilots were given this drug so they could fly long hours and not feel so bad about crashing into something at the end of their trip. . . . If you've ever wondered why someone would ever go through with a kamikaze mission, this may be one of your answers."[4]

Meth as Medicine

Today, methamphetamine is listed as a controlled substance by the US Drug Enforcement Administration (DEA). Meth, amphetamines, and other substances are included on one of five schedules based on factors such as therapeutic value, potential for abuse, and likelihood of addiction. Schedule I drugs, for instance, are those that the federal government deems to have no medically accepted use, are not considered safe even with medical supervision, and have high potential for abuse. Three examples of Schedule I drugs are heroin, ecstasy, and marijuana. Amphetamines and methamphetamine are Schedule II drugs, which are considered to have some therapeutic value but also a high potential for abuse.

Because it is classified as a Schedule II drug, meth can legally be prescribed by a physician. Under the brand name Desoxyn, for instance, meth in tablet form may be prescribed to treat the sleep disorder known as

> " **Because it is classified as a Schedule II drug rather than Schedule I, meth can legally be prescribed by a physician.** "

narcolepsy, attention-deficit hyperactivity disorder (ADHD), and some cases of obesity. Yet even though doses are significantly lower than those of street meth, the potential for abuse and addiction are so high that methamphetamine is seldom prescribed. Says Rob Bovett, the district attorney for Lincoln County, Oregon, and a methamphetamine expert: "I'm simply not aware of any doc that actually prescribes Desoxyn."[5]

The Rush and the High

All stimulant drugs rev up the central nervous system, but methamphetamine is often described as the most powerful—and the most addictive—of them all. It is not uncommon for someone to become addicted after using meth only once or twice. Dawn Johnston, who is a critical care flight nurse from West Michigan, explains: "It creates such an intense high that people, who have no thought of becoming addicted, dabble in it and become hooked because it's so potent."[6] When someone uses meth, adrenaline pours into the bloodstream and the brain is flooded with high amounts of dopamine, its primary pleasure chemical. This is a state of intense euphoria that is referred to as the rush. Drug addiction experts say that the rush from methamphetamine is at least three times as strong as the rush from cocaine and lasts much longer.

Next is the high phase, during which users become hyperactive and often develop exaggerated perceptions of their own strength and power.

It is typical for people who are high on meth to exhibit aggressive or bizarre behavior, as the Foundation for a Drug-Free World explains: "The abuser often feels aggressively smarter and becomes argumentative, often interrupting other people and finishing their sentences. The delusional effects can result in a user becoming intensely focused on an insignificant item, such as repeatedly cleaning the same window for several hours."[7] A meth high can last anywhere from six to twelve hours, which is significantly longer than the high of many other drugs, including cocaine.

When the High Wears Off

As exhilarating as a meth high may be, users must eventually come down from the high—and the experience is so bad that some cannot even describe it. This is known as the crash, and it happens because of chemical changes in the brain. After being bathed in artificially high levels of dopamine, the brain is now deprived of it, and its ability to naturally produce the chemical has been disrupted. This results in unbearable sadness and depression, as a former meth addict named Crystal explains: "The comedown is—HORRIBLE, the worst thing in the world, it's the worst depression you will ever have. All you want is to just, like, slit your wrists, you just want it to stop, just—anything. *Nothing* can make you feel happy; there's no comfort anybody can give you."[8]

> All stimulant drugs rev up the central nervous system, but methamphetamine is often described as the most powerful—and the most addictive—of them all.

The most dangerous stage of methamphetamine abuse is known as tweaking. Users are consumed by unbearable cravings, and all they can think about is getting more meth so they can be high again. They feel desperate and frustrated, and their behavior becomes unpredictable and erratic. This is when psychosis, the state of being out of touch with reality, is most common. The Foundation for a Drug-Free World explains: "The abuser is often in a completely psychotic state and he exists in his own world, seeing and hearing things that no one else can perceive. His hallucinations are so vivid that they seem real and, disconnected from reality, he can become hostile and dangerous to himself and others."[9]

Warning Signs of Meth Abuse

People who habitually use meth exhibit a number of telling symptoms. They are often anxious and fidgety, have a hard time sitting still, and become uncharacteristically talkative. Meth abusers commonly let themselves go, not showering or caring how they look; as a result, they develop a foul body odor. Drastic weight loss is another sign of repeated meth abuse. As users become more and more dependent on the drug, they forget to eat or lose interest in food altogether and become thin to the point of being emaciated.

Among the most obvious warning signs of habitual meth abuse is skin that is peppered with open sores. Meth users often obsessively pick at themselves because they are convinced that bugs are crawling on or under their skin. Clinical psychotherapist Robert Weiss refers to this as "meth lice" and says it causes addicts to "frantically scratch their face, arms, and legs with their fingernails—a behavior known as 'picking.'"[10]

Premature aging is another common symptom of habitual meth use. The skin sags and becomes pasty looking, covered with the sores and scabs of obsessive picking. The eyes look sunken and hollow, ringed by dark circles. Hair loses its luster and becomes thin and limp. The anti-meth group Life or Meth writes: "Just a few months abusing meth can physically age someone by ten years or more as they deteriorate into a zombie-like shell of their former self, akin to an internal light being snuffed out."[11]

From Soda Bottles to Superlabs

It is easy to understand why methamphetamine is so toxic just by knowing about the noxious stew of chemicals that are used to make it. The key ingredient is pseudoephedrine, a nasal decongestant in cold and allergy medications such as Sudafed. The tablets are crushed into a fine powder with a blender or coffee grinder. The powder is then combined with chemicals such as acetone (used in nail polish remover and paint thinner), heavy-duty drain cleaner, toluene (used in brake fluid), antifreeze, lantern fuel, and anhydrous ammonia (found in fertilizer). "As a chemist," says University of Oklahoma researcher Donna Nelson, "the idea

A California sheriff's department displays chemicals commonly used to make methamphetamine. Among the noxious ingredients that a meth lab might include in its product are acetone, used in nail polish remover and paint thinner; drain cleaner; toluene, used in brake fluid; and antifreeze.

of putting so many things with so many impurities in your body . . . I cringe at that."[12]

According to the DEA, an estimated 80 percent of the illicit methamphetamine in this country is manufactured in enormous meth laboratories known as "superlabs," most of which are located in Mexico. The remainder of the meth is produced in clandestine (secretive and hidden) labs that are scattered throughout the United States. These may be in home kitchens, garages, basements, and/or barns, and are often located in rural areas where law enforcement cannot easily find them.

Yet US meth labs are increasingly cropping up in cities and suburbs—and are not actually "labs" at all. Growing numbers of meth cooks are using a process known as the "one-pot" or "shake-and-bake" method to make small amounts of meth. This involves combining a handful of pseudoephedrine pills with chemicals in a large plastic bottle and then shaking it to ignite a chemical reaction. If done correctly, the cook can have meth in about an hour—but one wrong move and the bottle can explode into a massive fireball. Former meth addict and cook Robert Lucier explains: "It's like a small hydrogen bomb. It'll blow a hole . . . right through the floor, right through the ceiling, and then it'll just smoke everything out, turn everything black in a room."[13]

How Serious a Problem Is Methamphetamine Abuse?

According to a November 2012 US government report, 731,000 people in the United States aged twelve and older were current meth users in 2006, and by 2010 the number was 353,000—more than a 50 percent decline. As promising as this is, however, the numbers have begun to edge upward again, with 439,000 current meth users reported in 2011. In a July 2012 testimony, National Drug Control Policy director R. Gil Kerlikowske states: "Methamphetamine continues to be a drug of significant concern for both the public health and safety of many communities throughout the United States."[14]

Many law enforcement professionals and health officials agree that methamphetamine abuse is one of the country's most formidable drug problems. Largely because of the growth of shake-and-bake meth making, American cities and towns are plagued by meth abuse, and this presents a major challenge for law enforcement. One community where this is true is Montgomery County, Kansas, where Christopher Williams is a drug detective with the sheriff's office. "If you arrest one guy, chances are there are five guys down the street doing it," he says. "There's no shortage of people who are manufacturing methamphetamine."[15]

> **If done correctly, the cook can have meth in about an hour—but one wrong move and the bottle can explode into a massive fireball.**

What Are the Dangers of Methamphetamine Abuse?

Habitual use of methamphetamine can have disastrous effects on someone's health. The user often goes for days at a time without eating or sleeping, and between that and the pressure meth places on the central nervous system, the body takes a terrible beating. The increased heart

An anti-methamphetamine billboard being hung in Montana vividly illustrates one of the hazards of meth addiction: meth mouth. This condition is characterized by stained, rotting, and disintegrating teeth.

rate and blood pressure caused by meth use can cause severe damage to the user's heart, lungs, arteries, and liver. There is also risk of damaging the small blood vessels in the brain, which can lead to stroke.

One of the worst effects of long-term meth abuse is permanent brain damage. Studies have shown that repeated use of the drug can alter the wiring in the brain's pleasure centers, thereby destroying its ability to make dopamine. Eventually the user is unable to experience any pleasure at all, which is a devastating condition known as anhedonia. According to Weiss, this leads to an "ever deepening cycle of use and depression, and an increasing unwillingness to participate in life. Relationships disintegrate, jobs are lost. Children of crashing meth addicts are left to fend for themselves for days on end."[16]

Have Laws Reduced Methamphetamine Production and Use?

For years health officials, law enforcement personnel, and legislators have been searching for the most effective ways to fight the methamphetamine problem. In 2005 Congress passed the Combat Methamphetamine Epidemic Act (CMEA), which was signed into law by the president the following year. The CMEA was designed to cut down on meth production by regulating the sale of over-the-counter medications that contain pseudoephedrine. Retailers were required to place the products where customers did not have direct access to them, such as behind the counter. The law also limited the amount of pseudoephedrine products that any one customer could purchase each month.

> " Habitual use of methamphetamine can have disastrous effects on someone's health. "

After the CMEA was passed methamphetamine busts in the United States dropped drastically. The total number of clandestine lab incidents reported to the DEA fell from nearly 17,400 in 2003 to 7,347 in 2006—but within a few years, the number began climbing again. Meth producers learned how to get around the law through a practice known as "smurfing," whereby entire teams of people are hired to shop for pseudoephedrine products and buy their limit. In 2011 a man from Nashville, Tennessee, and his girlfriend were arrested and indicted for a smurfing operation. The couple had recruited more than three dozen people, including some who were homeless, to visit multiple pharmacies and purchase cold pills containing pseudoephedrine.

How Effective Are Prevention and Treatment Efforts?

People can and do recover from meth addiction, but overcoming it is extremely challenging—and most of those who are treated end up relapsing. Drug experts say that because meth is different from other drugs the key to recovery is extended time; therefore, a long-term approach to treatment is necessary. A report by the Tennessee District Attorneys General Conference explains: "The body needs more time to repair brain damage that occurs as a result of abuse. While drugs such as cocaine are quickly removed and almost completely metabolized in the body, meth has a longer duration of action, and a larger percentage of the drug remains unchanged in the body."[17]

> **People can and do recover from meth addiction, but overcoming it is extremely challenging—and most of those who are treated end up relapsing.**

The group goes on to offer a bleak prediction about methamphetamine recovery: "Users, police officers, doctors and families of users will tell you it's next to impossible to overcome meth addiction. For meth users undergoing current rehab programs, the success rate is very slim. With rates that low, the bottom line is simply don't start using."[18] This is where prevention programs come into play, one of which is the Meth Project. First launched in 2005, the program aims to significantly reduce methamphetamine use through provocative anti-meth advertising. In the states where it has been implemented, results have been impressive. In Montana, for instance, teenage meth use has dropped 63 percent since 2005, adult meth use has dropped by 72 percent, and meth-related crime has seen a 62 percent decline.

"The Most Evil Thing"

Methamphetamine is one of the most powerful and addictive drugs in existence. Meth causes an intense euphoric rush and a high that can last much longer than other drugs—followed by a crash that users describe as devastating. For a while, because of new laws that regulate pseudo-ephedrine, progress was being made in fighting the meth problem in the United States. But because of practices such as smurfing and shake-and-bake meth making, meth abuse is once again on the rise. Says Idaho State Police lieutenant Steve Davis, who has worked in narcotics for seventeen years: "This methamphetamine thing, it changes the dynamic of the work we do. It is the most evil thing I've seen in my career."[19]

How Serious a Problem Is Methamphetamine Abuse?

> **66**Law enforcement officials, drug counselors, and state legislators agree—there has never been a drug as powerful, addictive, and quick to destroy lives and communities as methamphetamine.**99**
>
> —Wyoming Meth Project, a prevention program aimed at reducing methamphetamine use through public service messaging, public policy, and community outreach.

> **66**Crystal methamphetamine, perhaps one of the most addictive and dangerous drugs in existence, has continuously plagued rural and urban regions of the country for the last three decades.**99**
>
> —Jeremy L. Williams, a policy analyst at the Council of State Governments' Southern office in Atlanta, Georgia.

McKinley Alkinani is a five-year-old boy from Salt Lake City, Utah, who suffers from a lung disease. To keep it under control he must take steroid medications every day and undergo regular breathing treatments. McKinley began to show symptoms of the condition when he was an infant, so his parents assumed he had been born with it. But because they had also developed severe health problems, they became suspicious—and were shocked to find out what was making them sick. The home they had purchased in a quiet, tree-lined neighborhood had formerly been a meth lab. Tests showed that the level of methamphetamine contamination was sixty-three times higher than the level at which the state department of health condemns a house. "We were constantly sick," says Jaimee Alkinani, McKinley's mother. "We blamed it on allergies and didn't think it could be our house."[20]

Toxic Homes

When methamphetamine cooks make the drug, the air is filled with toxic chemical fumes. Meth molecules cling to walls, floors, countertops, cabinets, and air ducts, as well as saturate carpets, drapes, and upholstery. The entire area where meth cooks produce their illicit concoction becomes contaminated and endangers the health of anyone who is exposed to it. Cleaning up these toxic messes is the specialty of Donetta Held, who owns a company in Indiana that decontaminates former meth labs. In her personal experience, the problem is growing worse. "Every year it's just happening more and more," says Held. "People are unknowingly purchasing new homes or renting apartments and saying, 'Wow, this was a former meth lab.' You can't always smell it and you can't always see it, but that doesn't mean it isn't there."[21]

In 2012 Scripps Howard News Service conducted an investigation. The team found that twenty-eight US states have laws that require home sellers or real estate agents to disclose information about meth lab contamination to prospective buyers. In many cases, however, if the home has been cleaned no disclosure is required—and in terms of getting rid of deadly toxins, the home may not be "clean" at all. This is what happened to the Alkinanis. After learning from a neighbor that their home had been a meth lab, they immediately called their realtor who said there was nothing to worry about. He assured them that the house had been decontaminated and even gave them a certificate from the health department to prove that the work had been done. The Alkinanis later discovered, however, that the person who was in charge of

> **The entire area where meth cooks produce their illicit concoction becomes contaminated and endangers the health of anyone who is exposed to it.**

the decontamination had rushed through the job and did not use the proper cleaning agents.

Children in Peril

Each year law enforcement professionals find thousands of meth labs in cities and towns throughout the United States. According to a 2012 report by the Office of National Drug Control Policy, US methamphetamine lab seizures grew from 3,100 in 2007 to nearly 6,400 in 2011—more than a 100 percent increase. Says agency director R. Gil Kerlikowske: "These domestic labs represent a major threat to public safety and the environment, as well as a significant burden on the already busy law enforcement officers responsible for locating and cleaning up these toxic labs."[22]

One of the biggest concerns associated with meth labs is the frequency with which children are affected by them. According to Kerlikowske, public safety officials often encounter situations where children have been directly exposed to these toxic environments. "Some children have dangerous chemicals or traces of illicit drugs in their systems," he says, "while others have suffered burns to their lungs or skin from chemicals or fire." Kerlikowske adds that the most disturbing cases are those where children have been injured in lab explosions and fires, "while others have been neglected or abused by adults living at lab sites."[23]

> **In the past, meth labs were nearly always tucked away in backwoods areas where law enforcement could not easily find them.**

That sort of tragedy occurred in February 2012, when a little boy from Akron, Ohio, died in a house that was being used as a meth lab. Patrick Lerch, who was seventeen months old, was living with his mother in a home where several men spent their time cooking meth and getting high. Patrick was badly neglected and left to fend for himself in the rat-infested basement where the meth lab was located. According to court documents, the little boy was forced to ingest meth on at least one occasion because he was crying. The medical examiner ruled that Patrick had died from methamphetamine poisoning, and his mother and the men involved were convicted and sent to prison. Prosecuting attorney Sherri Bevan Walsh shares her thoughts: "This was a horrific crime . . . Patrick's death is, unfortunately, a very sad example of how drugs—especially meth—ruin lives."[24]

The Changing Face of Meth Making

In the past, meth labs were nearly always tucked away in backwoods areas where law enforcement could not easily find them. These were often elaborate setups with chemistry paraphernalia such as rubber tubing and laboratory glassware in various shapes and sizes. Propane tanks, camp stoves or other types of heat sources, cookware, and a large array of chemical containers were also scattered about. As the meth cooked, a strong, smelly, ammonia-like odor wafted over a large area and was virtually impossible to conceal, which was why the labs could not be in neighborhoods or apartment buildings.

No one knows for sure who invented the one-pot method of meth production, which has been dubbed shake-and-bake. What is known, however, is that it changed everything. No longer does the process require a complex array of equipment, a fixed location, or even a heat source. With a handful of crushed pseudoephedrine tablets and a few different chemicals, a meth "lab" can be set up almost anywhere from a bathroom stall to a hotel room or the trunk of a car. Says Kevin Williams, who is sheriff in Marion County, Alabama: "It simplified the process so much that everybody's making their own dope. It can be your next-door neighbor doing it. It can be one of your family members living downstairs in the basement."[25]

> Although methamphetamine is made throughout the United States, the DEA says that an estimated 80 percent of the country's meth comes from Mexican superlabs.

In October 2012 a teacher at an elementary school in Murfreesboro, Tennessee, found the remnants of shake-and-bake meth making in a disturbing location—the school playground. While outside for recess with her first grade class, the teacher noticed a bag with a plastic bottle and tube lying on the ground. Although she did not know what it was, it looked suspicious to her, so she hustled her students back into the school and took the items to the assistant principal's office. The police arrived, investigators examined the contraption, and confirmed that it had been used to make meth. In a statement about the discovery police spokesman Kyle Evans said: "Meth labs are scary enough, but the fact that someone would bring one on a school campus is a dangerous situation."[26]

Meth Lab Hotspots

In January 2013 the DEA released a report of methamphetamine lab incidents for the calendar year 2012. These numbers represent the incidents that were reported by law enforcement to the DEA's El Paso Intelligence Center (EPIC) in 2012, including seizures of meth labs; waste material left behind at dump sites; and discovery of meth-making paraphernalia such as chemicals, glass, and equipment. The report showed that the five states with the most meth lab incidents in 2012 were Missouri with 1,825, Tennessee with 1,525, Indiana with 1,429, Kentucky with 919, and Illinois with 801.

> "Drug smuggling has also been a consistent problem in California border cities, and this has long presented challenges for law enforcement."

Indiana has struggled with methamphetamine abuse and meth lab activity for many years, and in areas throughout the state the problem is particularly bad. Evansville, an Indiana city located in the far southeast corner of the state, has had a long, difficult struggle with methamphetamine. An investigation conducted in 2012 by the Associated Press found that the Evansville area has seen a more than 500 percent increase in meth lab seizures since 2010.

Scott Hurt, an Evansville detective and member of the drug task force, says that Vanderburgh County (where Evansville is located) consistently leads the state in reported meth lab incidents. As with the rest of the state, Hurt says the problem in Evansville is largely caused by the tremendous growth of shake-and-bake meth making, and it is creating a risky situation for residents. He explains: "Because we're seeing the one-pots being manufactured in the city, in apartments, in neighborhoods, it is very dangerous for other members of the community."[27]

The Influx of Mexican Meth

Although methamphetamine is made throughout the United States, the DEA says that an estimated 80 percent of the country's meth comes from Mexican superlabs. In a report published in August 2011, the US Department of Justice National Drug Intelligence Center states that meth production in Mexico is "robust and stable, as evidenced by recent law enforcement reporting, laboratory seizure data, an increasing flow from Mexico, and a sustained upward trend in Mexican methamphetamine availability in U.S. markets."[28] The agency explains that Mexican drug trafficking organizations (known as cartels) are responsible for most meth that gets into the United States.

The 2011 report also says that the southwest border remains the primary gateway for moving illicit drugs into the United States. In Mexico methamphetamine is produced in enormous factorylike superlabs, as Associated Press journalist Jim Salter writes: "South of the border, meth is being made on an industrial scale. Sophisticated factories put out tons of the drug using formulas developed by professional chemists. The final product is often smuggled into the U.S. taped beneath tractor-trailers or hidden inside packages of other drugs."[29]

According to law enforcement officials in Tucson, Arizona, the city has virtually no meth labs—but not because people have stopped using the drug. Tucson is only about an hour's drive north of the Mexican border, and meth produced in superlabs comes into the city on a regular basis. Although there is no way to know with any certainty how much meth is successfully carried across the border, officials estimate that only a fraction of smugglers are ever caught.

Smugglers who have been nabbed at the border have used a number of creative methods in their attempts to get drugs into the United States. In February 2013, for example, border patrol officers found nearly $60,000 worth of bagged methamphetamine tucked inside two large buckets of fried chicken. That same month, crystal meth was discovered inside the lining of an ice chest that was partially filled with seafood. Says border patrol agent Crystal Amarillas: "They strap it to their body. They put it in the side of food bags, inside their luggage. They try different methods.

It's just a matter of getting adjusted to the trends and just being able to do our job and detect things."[30]

Drug smuggling has also been a consistent problem in California border cities, and this has long presented challenges for law enforcement. In December 2012 DEA agents completed an investigation called Operation Knight Stalker, which targeted Mexico's Knights Templar and La Familia Michoacán drug cartels. The twenty-one-month investigation resulted in the arrest of more than thirty cartel members who were trying to smuggle massive amounts of meth across the border into San Diego—and the bust netted more than 1,000 pounds (453.6 kg) of Mexican meth. In a news release, San Diego County district attorney Bonnie Dumanis expresses optimism about the results of the bust. "This operation gives you a window into the continuing large-scale drug trafficking that continues to plague San Diego County across the U.S.-Mexico border," Dumanis says. "The internal dynamics of these dangerous cartels is constantly changing, but operations like this one cripple their ability to do business."[31]

No End in Sight

From abandoned meth labs that sicken adults and children to the smuggled contraband of Mexico's massive superlabs, there is no doubt that methamphetamine is a serious problem in the United States. Some areas of the country have it worse than others, and meth making and abuse present an ongoing challenge for law enforcement. This is the case in Evansville, Indiana, where drug teams often feel they are making no headway. As Hurt explains: "The fact is, we are not winning this fight against methamphetamine."[32]

How Serious a Problem Is Methamphetamine Abuse?

❝ Unfortunately, the widespread availability of methamphetamine and other addicting drugs poses as great a threat today as anytime in our nation's history. ❞

—Ronald E. Brooks, "Statement for the Record," testimony before the US House of Representatives Committee on Oversight and Government Reform, July 24, 2012. http://oversight.house.gov.

Brooks is a retired assistant police chief and director of the Northern California High Intensity Drug Trafficking Area.

❝ Methamphetamine continues to pose a very significant threat to the health and safety of our citizens. ❞

—R. Gil Kerlikowske, testimony before the US House of Representatives Committee on Government Reform, *Meth Revisited: Review of State and Federal Efforts to Solve the Domestic Methamphetamine Production Resurgence*, July 24, 2012. www.whitehouse.gov.

Kerlikowske is director of the Office of National Drug Control Policy.

* Editor's Note: While the definition of a primary source can be narrowly or broadly defined, for the purposes of Compact Research, a primary source consists of: 1) results of original research presented by an organization or researcher; 2) eyewitness accounts of events, personal experience, or work experience; 3) first-person editorials offering pundits' opinions; 4) government officials presenting political plans and/or policies; 5) representatives of organizations presenting testimony or policy.

66 **Each year large quantities of illegal drugs are manufactured in the United States in clandestine drug
laboratories. Methamphetamine is the synthetic
drug most frequently produced in these clandestine
laboratories.** 99

—Drug Enforcement Administration (DEA), "The Drug Enforcement Administration's Clandestine Drug Laboratory Cleanup Program," June 2010. www.justice.gov.

An agency of the US Department of Justice, the DEA is the lead agency for domestic enforcement of federal drug laws and is also responsible for coordinating and pursuing US drug investigations abroad.

66 **Meth is a big problem here in California, and we need
to work together to win the war on this deadly drug.
. . . It wreaks havoc on families, increases crime, places
our children in danger and destroys the health of
citizens.** 99

—George Runner, "George Runner on How to Stop Meth in California," *Los Angeles Daily News*, May 22, 2012. www.dailynews.com.

Runner is a member of the California Board of Equalization and a former state senator.

66 **Unfortunately, history is once again repeating itself.
Law enforcement agencies across the country are reporting a disturbing trend—meth lab seizures are rising, and rising fast.** 99

—Joseph T. Rannazzisi, "The Status of Meth: Oregon's Experience Making Pseudoephedrine Prescription Only," statement before the US Senate Caucus on International Narcotics Control, April 13, 2010. www.justice.gov.

Rannazzisi is the deputy assistant administrator of the Drug Enforcement Administration's Office of Diversion Control.

66 **It is well known that meth addicts commonly engage
in conduct that, to those on the outside looking in, may
seem to defy logic, or in some cases, sanity.** 99

—Wayne Huffman, *Meth: A Memoir*. Berryville, AR: Midnight Express, 2012, p. 2.

Huffman is a former methamphetamine addict and producer (cook) who wrote this book while he was in prison.

“ Those who cook crystal meth in crystal meth labs are usually under the influence of the drug—not just when they’re cooking but all the time. This can mean some pretty shoddy decision making and potential negligence, an unsafe state in any situation but doubly so when volatile chemicals and heat are involved. ”

—Michael’s House, “Crystal Meth Labs and the Danger They Bring to the Neighborhood,” August 17, 2011. www.michaelshouse.com.

Michael’s House is a drug and alcohol treatment facility located in Palm Springs, California.

“ There are no drug kingpins in the world of meth lab manufacturing—only desperate addicts who cannot find a way to break the cycle of addiction. ”

—Jason Grellner, testimony before the US House of Representatives Committee on Oversight and Reform, *Meth Revisited: Review of State and Federal Efforts to Solve the Domestic Methamphetamine Production Resurgence*, July 24, 2012. http://oversight.house.gov.

Grellner is a detective sergeant and task force commander with the Franklin County Narcotics Enforcement Unit in Union, Missouri.

“ Environmentally toxic dump sites created by meth labs deflate property values and overwhelm medical services, often as a result of uninsured individuals seeking medical help. ”

—Office of National Drug Control Policy, “Methamphetamine Trends in the United States,” *Fact Sheet*, July 2010. www.whitehouse.gov.

The Office of National Drug Control Policy is responsible for directing the federal government’s antidrug programs.

Facts and Illustrations

How Serious a Problem Is Methamphetamine Abuse?

- According to the addiction treatment provider Elements Behavioral Health, an estimated **25 million people** worldwide are meth addicts, which is more than the total number of cocaine and heroin users combined.

- A 2011 report by the White House Office of National Drug Control Policy states that **methamphetamine laboratory incidents** nationwide, including labs, dump sites, and associated equipment, increased from 6,095 in 2007 to 11,239 in 2010.

- According to the National Institute on Drug Abuse, an estimated **13 million people** in the United States twelve years of age and older have used methamphetamine at some point in their lives.

- The California Bureau of Narcotics Enforcement estimates that at least **50 percent of pseudoephedrine** sold in California is being used in the illicit manufacture of methamphetamine.

- According to the National Congress of American Indians, **Alaskan Natives** and **American Indians** between eighteen and twenty-five years of age are as much as three times more likely to use methamphetamine than nonnatives.

Meth Use Less Prevalent than Other Drugs

Law enforcement and health officials consider methamphetamine abuse to be a formidable problem in the United States. However, when compared with other illicit drugs, meth ranks much lower in terms of use.

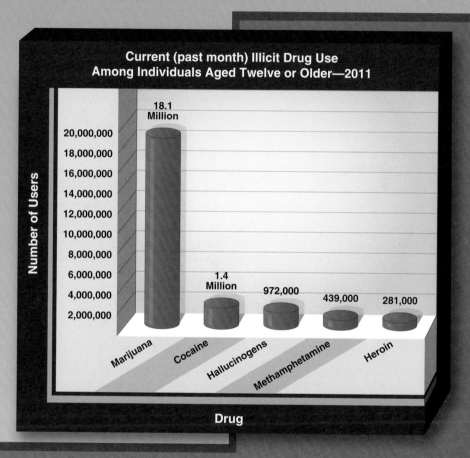

Current (past month) Illicit Drug Use Among Individuals Aged Twelve or Older—2011

Number of Users

- Marijuana: 18.1 Million
- Cocaine: 1.4 Million
- Hallucinogens: 972,000
- Methamphetamine: 439,000
- Heroin: 281,000

Drug

Source: Substance Abuse and Mental Health Services Administration (SAMHSA), "Results from the 2011 National Survey on Drug Use and Health Summary of National Findings," September 2012. www.samhsa.gov.

- In a July 2012 statement R. Gil Kerlikowske of the Office of National Drug Control Policy says that about **80 percent** of the methamphetamine labs seized in the United States are of the smallest capacity, producing less than 2 ounces (56.7 g).

Meth Use Is Declining Among Teens

Although law enforcement and health officials consider methamphetamine abuse to be a serious problem in the United States, teenage usage statistics are promising. As this graph shows, the percentage of teens who have used meth has declined significantly since 1999.

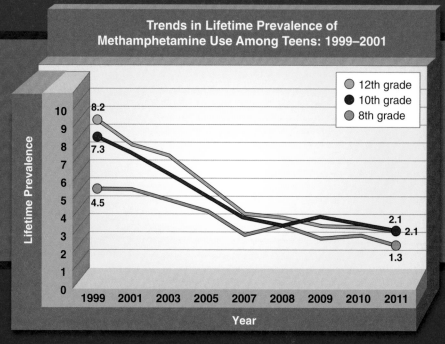

Trends in Lifetime Prevalence of Methamphetamine Use Among Teens: 1999–2001

Source: National Institute on Drug Abuse, "Monitoring the Future: National Results on Adolescent Drug Use," February 2012. www.monitoringthefuture.org.

- The US Department of Justice reports that **southwest border seizures** of methamphetamine in 2011 were more than twice the number seized in 2009.

- A July 2010 report by the White House Office of National Drug Control Policy states that methamphetamine lab incidents in Kentucky **more than doubled** from 2007 to 2009.

- A 2012 report by the United Nations Office on Drugs and Crime states that the number of **global methamphetamine seizures** in 2010 were more than double the amount in 2008.

Meth Labs Pose Dangers for All States

Wherever they are located, meth labs are potentially dangerous. The reaction caused by combining volatile chemicals can lead to explosion, resulting in severe burns and death. Also, the waste products left over from meth making are toxic to the environment. Although law enforcement throughout the United States is concerned about the dangers posed by meth labs, this map from the Drug Enforcement Administration (DEA) shows that the problem is worse in some states than others. Meth incidents, as defined by the DEA, include seizures of meth labs; waste material left behind at dump sites; and discovery of meth-making paraphernalia such as chemicals, glass, and equipment.

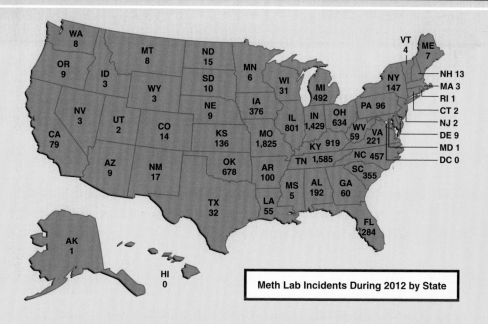

Meth Lab Incidents During 2012 by State

Source: Drug Enforcement Administration, "Methamphetamine Lab Incidents," 2004–2012, January 27, 2013. www.justice.gov.

- According to a November 2012 report by the Substance Abuse and Mental Health Services Administration, **133,000 people** in the United States were methamphetamine "initiates" during the previous month, meaning they used it for the first time.

What Are the Dangers of Methamphetamine Abuse?

66 Like other drugs, meth has deadly consequences, but it poses an additional threat: it is often made in a neighborhood home, leaving behind a toxic, poisonous mess that poses a danger to nearby families. 99

—L. Brooks Patterson, a business executive and former prosecutor from Michigan's Oakland County.

66 Methamphetamine's potent addiction liability and destructive health and social consequences make its abuse particularly dangerous. 99

—National Institute on Drug Abuse (NIDA), which seeks to end drug abuse and addiction in the United States.

When he looks back on his years as a methamphetamine addict, cook, and dealer, Mark Sullivan (not his real name) is filled with profound regret and sadness. Sullivan's life has been irreparably harmed by meth, and he has lost years that he knows he can never get back. As a direct result of cooking the drug, he suffers from a form of cancer known as Hodgkin's lymphoma. He taught his sister how to make meth, and after years of cooking and using the drug she died in 2010 from a combination of hepatitis, cancer, and diabetes. And then there are the awful memories. Even today he is still haunted by the crippling fear and paranoia that once dominated his life. "I was constantly consumed by suspicion," says Sullivan. "I repeatedly saw and heard things that weren't real."[33]

The Horrors of Psychosis

One incident in particular stands out in his mind. Sullivan had become convinced that one of his dealers, a man who had been his friend for ten years, was going to kill him. Day by day his paranoia continued to grow, and it resulted in an incident that almost turned tragic. One rainy night Sullivan heard a car pull into his driveway, and then he heard a man's voice say, "Let's search the house and find him."[34]

Certain that he was in grave danger, Sullivan grabbed his pistol, loaded it, and ran out of the house and into a dark alley. "I could hear footsteps behind me," he says. "My lungs burned." He broke into a house down the street from where he lived and hid in a laundry room with his gun cocked and ready, "waiting for them to come."[35] When Sullivan was confronted by the woman who lived in the house, he panicked and nearly shot her in the face. The only thing that kept him from pulling the trigger was her screaming, which startled him into realizing she was not the one who was after him.

Sullivan ran outside the house, terrified that his archenemy was right behind him. "I hid behind a bush down the street," he says, "sweating and clutching my gun." Then he noticed his girlfriend slowly driving by in his truck. "I jumped out of the bushes, ran into the street, and climbed in back, screaming, 'Go! Go! Go!' She hit the brakes and started crying." Sullivan's girlfriend had seen him run into the yard with the gun and had been driving around looking for him. "She told me no one ever came to the house," he says. "I had imagined it all."[36]

> **When meth abusers become psychotic, they often start compulsively picking and digging at their skin.**

What Sullivan experienced was psychosis, which involves paranoia and is a common side effect of heavy, repeated meth abuse. People who are psychotic cannot tell the difference between what is real and what is imaginary. They typically suffer from delusions, beliefs or fears that have no basis in reality; and hallucinations, hearing, seeing, and/or feeling things that do not actually exist. Alex Stalcup, a San Francisco physician who specializes in addiction, shares his thoughts about meth-induced psychosis: "Once people who are on meth become psychotic, they are very dangerous. They're completely bonkers; they're nuts. We're talking about very extreme alterations of normal brain function."[37]

When Paranoia Leads to Self-Mutilation

When meth abusers become psychotic, they often start compulsively picking and digging at their skin. Their paranoia may lead them to believe that bugs are crawling on them or have burrowed beneath the skin. They become convinced that the only way to get rid of the bugs is to dig them out, as the NIDA explains: "The person will pick or scratch, trying to get rid of the imaginary 'crank bugs.' Soon, the face and arms are covered with open sores that could get infected."[38]

Recovered meth addict Jeff Fowler will never forget the paranoia that led to his obsessive skin picking. One summer when he was in his twenties he went on a multiday meth binge and was feeling paranoid about almost everything. The weather was hot, the air was filled with gnats and flies, and when people went outside the insects landed on their skin. "Normally, that'd be pretty annoying," says Fowler. "When you're on speed and prone to paranoia, it was really bad." He became so convinced that his body had been infested by insects that he grabbed a razor-sharp box cutter and started digging it into his flesh. He explains: "I remember thinking, 'This is insane—you're cutting bugs out of your skin.' But I couldn't stop."[39]

> **Habitual meth use dries up the salivary glands; loss of saliva allows harsh acids and bacteria to build up on the gums, which causes cavities and rots teeth.**

A teenage boy named Ryan had a similar experience with meth-induced paranoia. His problem, though, was not bugs; Ryan was convinced that someone had implanted a computer chip in his big toe. He was determined to get it out so he grabbed a pair of needle-nose pliers and ripped off his toenail. "It is madness, it's insanity," says Ryan, who first used meth when he was twelve years old. "Logically you know there's nothing in there but you can't really distinguish the fantasy from reality so you'll sit there and pick at it and dig at it and try to get at it and sometimes you feel like it's moving and you're trying to chase it around, and sometimes it feels like it's burrowing deeper. I don't know, I can't even describe how much I hate meth. I wish it was never even invented."[40]

Meth Mouth

One of the most telltale signs that someone is a habitual methamphetamine abuser is bad gums and teeth, which is known as "meth mouth." The teeth of users who suffer from this condition become discolored and decayed and often rot and fall out. The American Dental Association explains: "Some users describe their teeth as 'blackened, stained, rotting, crumbling or falling apart.' Often, the teeth cannot be salvaged and must be removed."[41]

A number of factors contribute to the development of meth mouth, including neglected oral hygiene and poor nutrition. Regular use of methamphetamine shrinks blood vessels, thereby reducing the blood supply to the teeth and gums. This can lead to severe gum disease and infection. Another contributor is that meth users often clench their jaws and grind their teeth, which can cause teeth to crack and break. Also, habitual meth use dries up the salivary glands; loss of saliva allows harsh acids and bacteria to build up on the gums, which causes cavities and rots teeth. Meth users often attempt to remedy this "dry mouth" with soda and other sugary drinks, which fuels the growth of bacteria and leads to more tooth decay.

A teenage girl named Hailey, who started doing meth when she was fifteen, learned first-hand the effects of meth mouth. It happened one day while she was chewing gum. All of a sudden Hailey could feel little pieces of something that had gotten stuck in the gum—and when she pulled it out of her mouth, she found that the pieces were fragments of her tooth. "It just, like, crumbled," she says. "And so my back teeth are gone 'cause they just crumbled into bits and pieces."[42]

Scarred for Life

One of the reasons methamphetamine's popularity has been growing in recent years is the discovery of how easy it is to make using the shake-and-bake method—and over the same time period, increasing numbers of people are being rushed to the hospital after being severely burned. Jeffrey Guy, a physician at the Vanderbilt University Medical Center burn unit in Nashville, Tennessee, explains: "We're seeing people that are probably quite a bit more amateur methamphetamine producers. The burns are typically always involving the hands and the arms, and in the more severe cases, the chest, face and with severe inhalation injury."[43]

Several studies have examined the growing prevalence of burn injuries among people who make methamphetamine. One was a long-term study conducted by physicians at Bronson Methodist Hospital in Kalamazoo, Michigan, whose most recent findings were published in 2012. According to trauma surgeon Paul Blostein, a coauthor of the study, the team has found that not only is the number of burned patients increasing, but people who are burned while making meth typically have longer hospital stays and more expensive bills than other burn patients.

> **Dennis Potter is a recovering meth addict who was severely burned when his shake-and-bake 'lab' exploded in his face.**

The Bronson study also found that meth-related burn patients are more likely than other burn patients to suffer internal damage to the lungs and windpipe, to require a ventilator in order to breathe, and to have complications such as pneumonia, ulcers, and/or kidney problems. Blostein says the team has not been able to determine why the meth burn patients get sicker than other burn patients. He explains: "It may be some of the chemicals (used), the combustible substances—there are lots of ideas, but we can't say."[44]

Dennis Potter is a recovering meth addict who was severely burned when his shake-and-bake "lab" exploded in his face. Potter says that he had made meth the exact same way a thousand times without any problem. Then one night in December 2009 he was teaching the technique to a friend and something went wrong. Potter was holding the two-liter soda bottle in which he had mixed chemicals, and he suddenly noticed that the bottle had taken on an eerie orange glow. Within seconds there was an explosion so powerful that it blew out the room's walls and set Potter on fire: "My arms, my legs, my hair, my eyes—I was blind,"[45] he says. He spent the next five weeks in a hospital burn unit, wrapped in bandages and in terrible pain, and he underwent numerous skin graft operations—yet shortly after his discharge he went back to cooking meth again. "I wish I never learned how," says Potter, who is now trying to stay clean. "It haunts me daily because I do know how to do it."[46]

Risks to the Unborn

According to the March of Dimes, close to 4 percent of pregnant women in the United States have admittedly used cocaine, marijuana, methamphetamine, and/or other illicit drugs during their pregnancy. The group says that the use of meth by expectant mothers increases the risk of complications such as premature birth and placental problems. Birth defects are also a risk, as are low birth weight and smaller-than-normal head circumference. "The long-term outlook for these children is not known," says the March of Dimes. "Children who are born with low birthweight are at increased risk of learning and other problems. Children with reduced head circumference are more likely to have learning problems than those with low birthweight and normal head size. More studies are needed to determine the long-term outlook."[47]

Evaluating the effects of prenatal exposure to methamphetamine was the focus of a study led by Linda L. LaGasse, an associate professor of pediatrics at Brown University Medical School. For the study, which was published in April 2012, the researchers followed 330 children, of whom 166 had been exposed to methamphetamine before they were born. The children were evaluated at age three and again at age five. The team found that those whose mothers used meth were more emotionally reactive, anxious, and depressed at age three. At age five children in the methamphetamine exposure group were more likely to show aggressive behavior and symptoms of attention-deficit hyperactivity disorder (ADHD) than the comparison group. When the study was announced LaGasse stated: "These kids are not cracked and broken. But they do have problems that are worthy of note."[48]

> " **The list of dangers associated with methamphetamine is long and scary.** "

The Drug of Nightmares

The list of dangers associated with methamphetamine is long and scary. Psychosis can make users believe that people are out to get them or that their skin has been infested with bugs. Meth mouth destroys people's gums and teeth. For users who cook their own meth, the danger of severe burns—and possibly death—is very real. Meth is a drug that has so many terrible side effects and dangers that many users wish they had never even heard of it. Fowler shares his thoughts: "It's a nightmare. That thing that starts off seeming so cool and fun turns into a nightmare, but by the time you realize it's a nightmare, you can't even care anymore."[49]

What Are the Dangers of Methamphetamine Abuse?

❝ Besides being addictive, repeated or continuous methamphetamine use can cause heart damage, erosion and decay of the teeth and severe mental disorders. ❞

—Narconon International, "Methamphetamine Abuse," 2012. www.narconon.org.

Narconon International helps people who are addicted to drugs by providing educational information and rehabilitation programs.

❝ The chemicals as well as the vapors and fumes created in the production of crystal meth are highly flammable. Fires and explosions are very common—a threat to those in the meth lab as well as neighbors and anyone else in the vicinity. ❞

—Michael's House, "Risks of Crystal Meth Use and Addiction," October 5, 2011. www.michaelshouse.com.

Michael's House is a drug and alcohol treatment facility located in Palm Springs, California.

66 Methamphetamine users expose themselves to risk of HIV infection through injection and unsafe sexual practices. 99

—Miriam Boeri, *Women on Ice: Methamphetamine Use Among Suburban Women*. New Brunswick, NJ: Rutgers University Press, 2013, p. 15.

Boeri is an associate professor of sociology and criminal justice at Kennesaw State University in Kennesaw, Georgia.

66 In high doses, this drug can cause hyperthermia, convulsions and death. 99

—Royal Canadian Mounted Police, "Crystal Meth, What You Need to Know," December 30, 2011. www.rcmp-grc.gc.ca.

The Royal Canadian Mounted Police is the Canadian national police service and an agency of Canada's Ministry of Public Safety.

66 Methamphetamine abuse leads to devastating medical, psychological, and social consequences. 99

—Wyoming Meth Project, "About Methamphetamine," 2012. http://wyoming.methproject.org.

The Wyoming Meth Project is a prevention program aimed at reducing methamphetamine use through public service messaging, public policy, and community outreach.

66 The raw materials and waste of the meth labs pose environmental dangers because they are often disposed of indiscriminately by lab operators to avoid detection. 99

—US Government Accountability Office (GAO), *Drug Control: State Approaches Taken to Control Access to Key Methamphetamine Ingredient Show Varied Impact on Domestic Drug Labs*, January 2013. www.gao.gov.

The GAO is an independent, nonpartisan watchdog agency that reports to Congress and investigates how the federal government spends taxpayer dollars.

“Ten years ago, I was diagnosed with Hodgkin's disease as a direct result of cooking meth.”

—Mark Sullivan, "The Real 'Breaking Bad': Confessions of a Former Meth King," *Newsweek Daily Beast*, July 16, 2011. www.thedailybeast.com.

Sullivan is a former methamphetamine addict and dealer who writes under an assumed name as he works to rebuild his life.

“Methamphetamine can cause significant visual hallucinations, violent behavior, paranoia and confusion that far exceed the degrees of negative side effects from other common illegal drugs.”

—Jeremy L. Williams, "The Resurgence of Crystal Meth: Trends and State Responses," *Book of the States*, Council of State Governments, 2011. http://knowledgecenter.csg.org.

Williams is a policy analyst at the Council of State Governments in Atlanta, Georgia.

“Long-term methamphetamine abuse can cause addiction, anxiety, insomnia, mood disturbances, and violent behavior.”

—Office of National Drug Control Policy, "Methamphetamine Trends in the United States," *Fact Sheet*, July 2010. www.whitehouse.gov.

A component of the Executive Office of the President, the Office of National Drug Control Policy is responsible for directing the federal government's antidrug programs.

Facts and Illustrations

What Are the Dangers of Methamphetamine Abuse?

- According to the National Institute on Drug Abuse, chronic methamphetamine abuse significantly changes how the **brain functions**.

- A study published July 2012 by researchers Scott Cunningham and Keith Finlay found that the increase in methamphetamine abuse throughout the United States has resulted in a significant rise in **child abuse and neglect**.

- According to Indiana State Police investigators Chip Ayers and Jeremy Franklin, every pound (.45 kg) of meth that is produced leaves behind up to 6 pounds (2.72 kg) of **toxic waste** that can cost tens of thousands of dollars to clean up.

- The US Department of Justice states that approximately **15 percent** of meth labs are discovered as a result of fire or explosion.

- According to the White House Office of National Drug Control Policy, **psychosis** can persist for months or even years after methamphetamine use has ceased.

- Ronald E. Brooks, president of the national Narcotic Officers' Association coalition, states that in communities where meth is prevalent, as much as **85 percent** of the child abuse and endangerment is attributed to methamphetamine use.

Meth Use Has Damaging Effects

People who habitually use methamphetamine can damage their physical and mental health—both short-term and long-term. The effects range from appetite loss to brain damage.

Short-term effects of methamphetamine	Long-term effects of methamphetamine
Loss of appetite	Permanent damage to blood vessels of heart and brain
Increased heart rate and blood pressure, shortness of breath	High blood pressure leading to heart attacks, strokes, and death
Elevated body temperature, profuse sweating	Damage to kidneys, liver, and lungs
Disturbed sleep patterns/Insomnia	Destruction of tissues in nose if snorted
Nausea and vomiting	Respiratory (breathing) problems if snorted
Bizarre, erratic, sometimes violent behavior	Infectious diseases and abscesses if injected
Hallucinations, hyperexcitability, irritability	Severe tooth decay
Panic and psychosis (paranoia)	Psychosis
Convulsion, seizures, risk of death from high doses	Strong psychological dependence (addiction), depression
	Damage to the brain similar to Alzheimer's disease, stroke, and epilepsy

Source: Foundation for a Drug-Free World, "The Deadly Effects of Meth," [undated]. www.drugfreeworld.org.

- According to Joanna Fowler, a chemist at Brookhaven National Laboratory, the **surge of dopamine** that occurs when someone uses methamphetamine is so strong that it damages the brain's dopamine system.

Severe Burns from Meth Labs

Some methamphetamine users have discovered the technique known as one-pot or shake-and-bake meth making. With this risky practice, someone can have meth in less than an hour—but one wrong move and the mini-lab can explode in the person's face. A study published in February 2013 by a team of critical care physicians from Bronson Methodist Hospital in Kalamazoo, Michigan, found that between 2008 and 2010 the growth of shake-and-bake meth making in the state led to a corresponding spike in severe burn injuries.

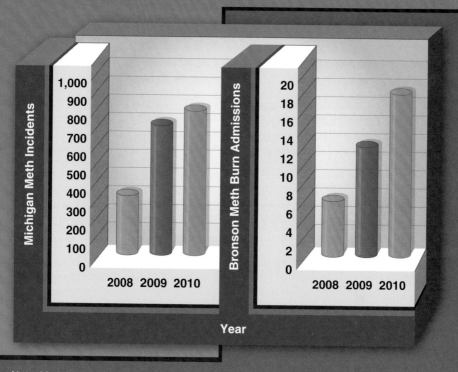

Note: Meth lab incidents include seizures of meth labs; waste material left behind at dump sites; and discovery of meth-making paraphernalia such as chemicals, glass, and equipment.

Source: Scott B. Davidson et al., "Resurgence of Methamphetamine Related Burns and Injuries: A Follow-Up Study," *Burns*, February 2013, pp. 199–225.

- The Foundation for a Drug-Free World states that meth quickly creates **dependence** in users that can only be relieved by taking more of the drug.

- According to the Meth Project, methamphetamine causes **increased heart rate** and **blood pressure** that can lead to irreversible damage to blood vessels in the brain, which increases the risk of stroke.

- Joanna Fowler, a chemist at Brookhaven National Laboratory, says that long-term methamphetamine use destroys the **frontal cortex**, which is the brain's judgment center, and this can lead to bad decision making.

- According to the National Institute on Drug Abuse, neuroimaging studies have shown that function in some regions of the brain **does not display recovery** even after two years of abstinence, which indicates that some meth-induced changes are very **long lasting and possibly permanent.**

- The Meth Project says that the reduced dopamine levels caused by methamphetamine abuse can result in symptoms that resemble those of **Parkinson's disease**, a severe brain disorder that involves tremors (shaking) and difficulty with walking, movement, and coordination.

Have Laws Reduced Methamphetamine Production and Use?

> **Methamphetamine is becoming easier to make and existing meth laws are becoming easier to circumvent.**
>
> —Jeremy L. Williams, a policy analyst at the Council of State Governments in Atlanta, Georgia.

> **Despite federal and state pseudoephedrine sales restrictions in the United States, the overall incidence of smurfing has increased, facilitating the concurrent rise in domestic methamphetamine production.**
>
> —US Department of Justice, the United States' primary criminal investigation and law enforcement agency.

In December 2011 Tulsa, Oklahoma, journalist Wayne Greene met with a group of eleven recovering methamphetamine users. Most of them said they were meth cooks as well as users, and nearly all had been in prison at least once for drug-related offenses. Among the topics of discussion was a law that was being considered by the Oklahoma legislature that would make pseudoephedrine available only with a doctor's prescription. Several members of the group were strongly in favor of such a law, including Gayla Payne. She has been clean from meth for four years and is convinced that the law would help curb meth abuse, as she told Greene: "I think that is the best idea I've ever heard."[50]

A Meth Epidemic

Medications containing pseudoephedrine became available for over-the-counter (OTC) purchase in 1976. Following an extensive, long-term study known as a monograph, the Food and Drug Administration (FDA) approved pseudoephedrine products for sale as decongestants. The OTC rating ensured that the drugs could be purchased without oversight by a health care professional. Rob Bovett refers to the FDA's action as "inadvertently letting the genie out of the bottle." Once meth cooks throughout the United States became aware of pseudoephedrine's availability, says Bovett, "the meth epidemic spread across the nation, leaving destroyed lives and families in its wake."[51]

Many legislators and law enforcement professionals agreed with Bovett that the United States was suffering from a methamphetamine epidemic and that it was growing worse. Statistics compiled by the DEA showed that in 1999 (the first year such data were tracked) there were fewer than 7,000 methamphetamine lab incidents nationwide, and by 2004 the number had soared to 23,829. Congress passed several laws in the 1980s and 1990s to help curb the growth of methamphetamine abuse and production, but the problem continued to escalate. Ronald E. Brooks, a retired assistant police chief and director of the Northern California High Intensity Drug Trafficking Area, recalls what a tumultuous time it was:

> While the definition of "lab incidents" at the time was interpreted differently depending on jurisdiction, more than 50 meth lab incidents *per day* were occurring in this country, and the number of states reporting a major meth lab problem had greatly increased. We were inundated—it was truly an "epidemic." Toxic waste was being discovered in local water sources. Maimed and burned people—including children—from meth lab explosions were becoming more common.[52]

Tightening Controls

In an attempt to get a handle on the country's worsening meth problem, the US Congress passed the Combat Methamphetamine Epidemic Act (CMEA) in 2005. The legislation, which then-president George W. Bush signed into law the following year, established new restrictions on over-the-counter medications that contained pseudoephedrine. These drugs were targeted because it was well known to law enforcement that massive quantities were being purchased specifically to be turned into meth. Says Brooks: "We needed to make it much more difficult for meth cooks to access the most important ingredient: pseudoephedrine."[53]

The new law mandated that drugs with pseudoephedrine would be kept behind the counter or in a locked cabinet where customers did not have direct or easy access to them. Limits were placed on the number of pseudoephedrine products customers could buy in a thirty-day time period. In addition, customers were required to sign a logbook and show photo identification before they could buy the medications, and retailers were required to maintain a written record of pseudoephedrine product purchases.

> " Congress passed several laws in the 1980s and 1990s to help curb the growth of methamphetamine abuse and production, but the problem continued to escalate. "

The effects of the CMEA were obvious almost immediately. Since meth cooks no longer had easy access to whatever quantities of pseudoephedrine products they wanted to buy, meth lab incidents began to decline. DEA reports show, for instance, that by 2007 the number of reported meth lab incidents had dropped to 6,858 from the 23,829 total three years before. Says Joseph T. Rannazzisi, who is deputy assistant administrator of the DEA's Office of Diversion Control: "Meth lab incidents plummeted and proved that effective chemical control could have a dramatic positive impact on illicit methamphetamine production."[54]

Short-Lived Progress

The positive effects of the CMEA did not last very long, however. By 2008 the number of meth lab incidents had started to climb again and continued to increase each year after that. The problem affected almost all US states, but some were hit particularly hard. Mississippi, for instance, had 178 meth lab incidents in 2007, and two years later the number had risen to 938. According to Marshall Fisher, who is executive director of the Mississippi Bureau of Narcotics, it was the highest number of lab incidents ever recorded in the state. He explains: "Methamphetamine-related arrests exceeded the combined total of both powder and crack cocaine arrests for the first time in Mississippi drug law enforcement history. Of approximately 3,000 drug arrests for 2009, nearly one-third were methamphetamine related."[55]

The effectiveness of the CMEA was short-lived for several reasons, one of which was the fast-growing shake-and-bake method of meth production. Since it used a fraction of the pseudoephedrine that was required for a traditional meth lab, small-time users could make the drug for their own use without being hindered by the limitations of the federal law. Says Mark Woodward, spokesman for the Oklahoma Bureau of Narcotics and Dangerous Drugs Control: "Somebody somewhere said 'Wait, this requires a lot less pseudoephedrine, and I can fly under the radar.'"[56]

> **Meth cooks quickly figured out that if they were not able to buy their required supply of pseudoephedrine products, they could just hire people to do it for them.**

Another factor that considerably weakened the CMEA's effectiveness was the advent of smurfing. Meth cooks quickly figured out that if they were not able to buy their required supply of pseudoephedrine products, they could just hire people to do it for them. Robert Lucier ran a gang of what he calls "super smurfers," and explains how the operation worked: "People go inside and purchase these items for you in small quantities, and you just take them around to all these different stores. And you just buy one or two boxes, you know, and you have four or five people, and you just go from town to town, loading up the trunk with boxes of pills."[57]

Today, smurfing is more prolific than ever. Meth cooks hire all kinds of people to be smurfers, from family members to addicts who exchange their services for drugs. Many jump at the chance to smurf because they can earn a lot of money for relatively little work—but what they are doing is a crime that carries stiff penalties if they get caught. Linda Clark, a sixty-year-old grandmother from Jonesboro, Arkansas, found this out the hard way. Between 2010 and 2012 Clark drove across the border into Tennessee and purchased a large quantity of pseudoephedrine products. She paid ten dollars per package and was able to sell them to meth cooks for fifty dollars. She was caught and charged with promotion of manufacturing methamphetamine, which is a felony offense that could lead to a prison sentence.

Electronic Tracking

Most states have passed some kind of anti-meth legislation, and these laws have had mixed results. In 2006, for instance, Oklahoma became the first state to require tracking through an electronic system developed by the state's Bureau of Narcotics. This technology allowed pharmacies to instantly verify whether a buyer had already purchased his or her legal limit of pseudoephedrine. Later that same year Tennessee implemented a similar system, and Kentucky followed suit in 2008. By 2012 twenty states had electronic tracking systems in place.

> **In 2005 government officials in Oregon took the boldest step of any US state in their fight against methamphetamine.**

According to a January 2013 report by the US Government Accountability Office (GAO), electronic systems are beneficial in helping to enforce pseudoephedrine sales limits. The report states: "By electronically automating and linking log-book information on PSE sales, these systems can block individuals from purchasing more than allowed by law. In addition, electronic tracking systems can help law enforcement investigate potential PSE diversion, find meth labs, and prosecute individuals." The GAO goes on to say, however, that tracking systems have not been effective in reducing meth lab incidents: "Meth cooks have been able to limit the effectiveness of such systems as a means to reduce diversion through the practice of smurfing."[58]

Fisher, who spent more than thirty years in law enforcement and is a former DEA agent, is convinced that electronic tracking systems are not effective. He points out several flaws, one of which is the number of law enforcement resources the systems require in order to operate. "The cost of implementing an electronic log system," says Fisher, "would not significantly offset the costs of methamphetamine abuse." He adds that meth cooks are savvy enough to know how to get around these systems. "Electronic tracking does *not* block false identifications and does not stop the multiple numbers of smurfers—thus rendering electronic logs ineffective."[59]

By Prescription Only

In 2005 government officials in Oregon took the boldest step of any US state in their fight against methamphetamine. Legislators passed a bill that made pseudoephedrine available only with a doctor's prescription. Bovett, who was the primary author of the legislation, is convinced that such a strong approach is the only way to effectively address the problem of pseudoephedrine being diverted for illegal meth production. Bovett refers to the laws that have been passed throughout the years as "Band-Aids," saying that Oregon finally decided that a bold move was long overdue. "We got tired of putting Band-Aids on the situation and watching the smurfers and the meth cooks get around it," says Bovett, "so we just simply decided to return pseudoephedrine to a prescription drug, which is what it was before 1976, and we ended the problem."[60]

The results of Oregon's anti-meth legislation have been dramatic. According to the Oregon Narcotics Enforcement Association, the number of meth lab incidents in the state plummeted from 473 in 2003 to just 7 in 2012—and during nine months of 2012, there were no meth lab incidents reported at all. "In addition," says policy analyst Jeremy L. Williams, "the state's property crime rate, which has a direct correlation to methamphetamine use, declined by approximately 17 percent in 2006, the largest decrease in the country."[61]

In 2010 Mississippi followed Oregon's lead and passed legislation that also made pseudoephedrine products available by prescription only. As with Oregon, the law resulted in a significant reduction in methamphetamine lab incidents. "While we still have some labs in Mississippi," says Fisher, "we have seen a drastic reduction in their numbers and size, and the only thing Mississippi did differently was to schedule pseudoephedrine." By "scheduling," Fisher means that pseudoephedrine has been added to the state's list of Schedule III controlled substances, or those that require a doctor's prescription for purchase. He goes on to say: "As a law enforcement officer with more than three decades of experience, twenty-nine years of which has been in narcotics, the scheduling of pseudoephedrine in Mississippi may be our most effective piece of law enforcement legislation in the last 30 years."[62]

> Making pseudoephedrine available by doctor's prescription only would be a radical move that has numerous opponents, which means the issue is not likely to be resolved anytime soon.

At the end of his statement, which was given in July 2012 before a subcommittee of the US House of Representatives, Fisher offered his recommendation for America's ongoing struggle with methamphetamine abuse, production, and distribution: "I can only hope that our nation is able to get a grasp on this problem and that we pursue the only viable solution, which is to schedule pseudoephedrine on a national level."[63] Many in law enforcement, including Bovett, as well as a number of legislators and antidrug groups, agree wholeheartedly with Fisher's recommendation—but not everyone does. Making pseudoephedrine available by doctor's prescription only would be a radical move that has numerous opponents, which means the issue is not likely to be resolved anytime soon.

Uncertainty Lingers

The United States continues to struggle with its methamphetamine problem. A federal law that attempted to resolve it by making pseudoephedrine harder to obtain was effective for a few years, as were state electronic tracking systems. These measures lost their effectiveness, however, when meth cooks discovered the shake-and-bake method and then learned about the convenience of smurfing. A growing number of people are supportive of a federal law that mirrors what Oregon and Mississippi have done, but this is an issue of controversy that will likely be debated for years before any action is taken—if that ever happens at all.

Primary Source Quotes*

Have Laws Reduced Methamphetamine Production and Use?

66 **The only effective solution is to put the genie back in the bottle by returning pseudoephedrine to prescription-drug status. That's what Oregon did more than four years ago, enabling the state to eliminate smurfing and nearly eradicate meth labs.** 99

—Rob Bovett, "How to Kill the Meth Monster," *New York Times*, November 15, 2010. www.nytimes.com.

Bovett is the district attorney for Lincoln County, Oregon, and the primary author of the state's stringent anti-methamphetamine law.

66 **What Rob Bovett actually demands, then, is that people sacrifice cheap, safe, and effective medicine so he and like-minded authoritarians can look like they are fighting drug abuse.** 99

—Jacob Sullum, "Speed 5: This Time for Sure," *Reason Hit and Run*, blog, November 16, 2010. http://reason.com.

Sullum is senior editor at *Reason* magazine and a nationally syndicated columnist.

Bracketed quotes indicate conflicting positions.

* Editor's Note: While the definition of a primary source can be narrowly or broadly defined, for the purposes of Compact Research, a primary source consists of: 1) results of original research presented by an organization or researcher; 2) eyewitness accounts of events, personal experience, or work experience; 3) first-person editorials offering pundits' opinions; 4) government officials presenting political plans and/or policies; 5) representatives of organizations presenting testimony or policy.

Primary Source Quotes

66 Thanks to the Combat Methamphetamine Epidemic Act in 2005, today there are restrictions on the purchase of over-the-counter products containing pseudoephedrine. . . . But illegal drug manufacturers have found ways to circumvent this law. **99**

—Dianne Feinstein, "Senate Caucus on International Narcotics Control Holds Hearing on Methamphetamine and Making Pseudoephedrine Prescription Only," US Senate Caucus on International Narcotics Control, April 13, 2010. http://drugcaucus.senate.gov.

Feinstein is a United States Senator from California.

66 Oregon's prescription-only law has resulted in fewer meth lab incidents in that state. **99**

—Office of National Drug Control Policy, "Methamphetamine Trends in the United States," *Fact Sheet*, July 2010. www.whitehouse.gov.

A component of the Executive Office of the President, the Office of National Drug Control Policy is responsible for directing the federal government's antidrug programs.

66 The prescription requirement for cold and allergy medicines containing pseudoephedrine had no more of an impact on the reduction of meth lab incidents than other measures adopted in neighboring states. **99**

—Steve Buckstein, "Requiring a Prescription for Cold Medicine Has Not Reduced Meth Use in Oregon," press release, Cascade Policy Institute, February 21, 2012. http://cascadepolicy.org.

Buckstein is senior policy analyst at the Cascade Policy Institute in Portland, Oregon.

66 Our current 'war on drugs' policy framework is in large part either ineffective or, worse, counterproductive. **99**

—Howard Rahtz, *Drugs, Crime, and Violence*. Lanham, MD: Hamilton, 2012, p. 2.

Rahtz is a retired police captain from Cincinnati, Ohio.

66 It is because of meth that there are limits on the amount of cold medicine you are legally permitted to purchase and possess. That law, since its creation, has done little to slow meth production, especially when the law hasn't been enforced equally in all areas of the United States. 99

—Wayne Huffman, *Meth: A Memoir*. Berryville, AR: Midnight Express, 2012, p. 3.

Huffman is a former methamphetamine addict and producer (cook) who wrote this book while he was in prison.

66 A certain portion of society will, regardless of legal restrictions and enforcement, choose to use drugs. So the solution is quite simple, really: end the drug war. Less enforcement and lower penalties would reduce the price of marijuana and shift demand from crystal meth back to marijuana, a drug that has few of the problems associated with meth. 99

—Mark Thornton, "What Explains Crystal Meth?," *Mises Daily*, January 20, 2011. http://mises.org.

Thornton is a senior resident fellow at the Auburn, Alabama, think tank Ludwig von Mises Institute.

Have Laws Reduced Methamphetamine Production and Use?

- According to Lincoln County, Oregon, district attorney Rob Bovett, since 2006 when Oregon passed legislation making products containing ephedrine and pseudoephedrine available by **prescription only**, the rate of meth lab incidents has dropped by **96 percent**.

- Nearly sixty Missouri communities have adopted laws that require **prescriptions to buy pseudoephedrine**, such as Cape Girardeau County; according to a February 2012 article in the *Daily Statesman* newspaper, the region has seen a 30 percent drop in meth-related incidents.

- In 2004 Oklahoma was the first state to reclassify pseudoephedrine as a **Schedule V controlled substance** and impose restrictions on the sale of products that contain it.

- The Mississippi Bureau of Narcotics says that methamphetamine lab busts in the state dropped nearly **70 percent** in the eight months following the passage of legislation making pseudoephedrine available by prescription only.

- In an April 2012 report Patricia R. Freeman and Jeffery Talbert of the Institute for Pharmaceutical Outcomes and Policy say that the majority of states have enacted laws controlling the sale of products containing **pseudoephedrine and ephedrine** that are more stringent than current federal law.

Oregon Law Reduces State's Meth Lab Incidents

In 2006 Oregon took the boldest step of any state in its fight against methamphetamine by passing a law that made pseudoephedrine (a key ingredient in meth) available only with a doctor's prescription. Since then meth incidents* in Oregon have declined.

Oregon Meth Lab Incidents: 2004 to 2012

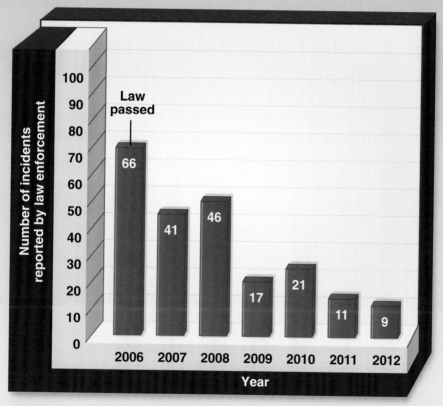

*Meth lab incidents include seizures of meth labs; waste material left behind at dump sites; and discovery of meth-making paraphernalia such as chemicals, glass, and equipment.

Source: Drug Enforcement Administration, "Methamphetamine Lab Incidents, 2004–2012, January 27, 2013. www.justice.gov.

Little Public Support for Federal Pseudoephedrine Law

Antidrug organizations and many law enforcement professionals support a federal law that would make medications containing pseudoephedrine (needed for making methamphetamine) available only through a doctor's prescription. However, a February 2013 poll by the Asthma and Allergy Foundation of America found little support for such a law among survey respondents.

Participant responses when asked whether a federal law should be passed to require a doctor's prescription for purchase of medications containing pseudoephedrine

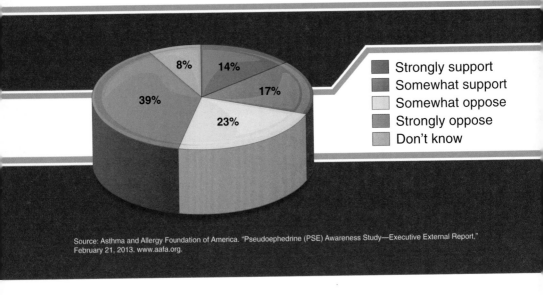

8%   14%   17%   39%   23%

- Strongly support
- Somewhat support
- Somewhat oppose
- Strongly oppose
- Don't know

Source: Asthma and Allergy Foundation of America. "Pseudoephedrine (PSE) Awareness Study—Executive External Report," February 21, 2013. www.aafa.org.

- A 2013 report by the Government Accountability Office states that in 2011, **electronic tracking systems** were used to block the sale of more than 480,000 boxes and 1,142,000 grams of pseudoephedrine products in eleven states.

- According to a February 2012 article in the *Daily Statesman* newspaper, after Scott County, Missouri, passed legislation to restrict the sale of pseudoephedrine, its meth-related incidents dropped more than **50 percent**.

Meth Cooks Not Deterred by Electronic Tracking

Electronic tracking is aimed at preventing people from buying more pseudo-ephedrine products (needed for making methamphetamine) than is allowed by law. According to the US Government Accountability Office (GAO), meth lab incidents* have not declined in states that use electronic tracking. In the three states that have used this system the longest, meth lab incidents dropped between 2004 and 2006, probably related to federal pseudoephedrine sales restrictions. But the number of incidents has risen since 2007, in part because of smurfing (multiple individuals travel from store to store to buy pseudo-ephedrine products) and the shake-and-bake method of meth production.

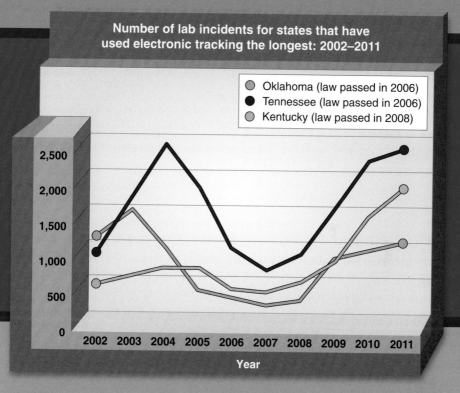

Number of lab incidents for states that have used electronic tracking the longest: 2002–2011

Oklahoma (law passed in 2006)
Tennessee (law passed in 2006)
Kentucky (law passed in 2008)

*Meth lab incidents include seizures of meth labs; waste material left behind at dump sites; and discovery of meth-making paraphernalia such as chemicals, glass, and equipment.

Source: Government Accountability Office, "Drug Control: State Approaches Taken to Control Access to Key Methamphetamine Ingredient Show Varied Impact on Domestic Drug Labs," January 2013. www.gao.gov.

- Lincoln County, Oregon, district attorney Rob Bovett states that since 2006, when Oregon passed legislation making products containing ephedrine and pseudoephedrine available by prescription only, the number of meth-related arrests has declined **32 percent**.

How Effective Are Prevention and Treatment Efforts?

66 **We know any approach to addressing our nation's drug problem, including the use and abuse of methamphetamine, must include prevention, treatment, and recovery.** 99

—Jason Grellner, a detective sergeant and task force commander with the Franklin County Narcotics Enforcement Unit in Union, Missouri.

66 **People hoping to get sober from meth are in a state of physical and mental vulnerability, and meth is simply too strong. Drug rehab is the only effective way to get free from a meth addiction.** 99

—Michael's House, a drug and alcohol treatment facility located in Palm Springs, California.

After four years of using crystal meth, it took a devastating tragedy for Kiyana Geske to finally get clean. Her fiancé, who was also a meth addict, died from an overdose. From that day on Geske vowed to stay away from the drug, and she has done so. Today she uses her experience to help kids understand the dangers of meth by volunteering with the Colorado Meth Project. She goes to high schools throughout southern Colorado and speaks to students about what she went through. She tells them how easy it is to get addicted to meth by sharing what happened when she tried the drug for the first time. "I stayed up for four days," says Geske, "and coming down was so hard. I was physically in pain, I was paranoid, I hadn't slept, I felt sick to my stomach. So I decided I'd take a little bit more."[64]

Geske is honest with the students about how she spent the next four years hopelessly hooked on meth. She lost her friends and her family and lived for nothing but getting high. "I was living in apartments of other meth addicts," she says, "just jumping from couch to couch, sleeping behind grocery stores."[65] It was not until her fiancé died that she started to get her life back together, and now she wants to give back by helping other young people.

The Shock Factor

When Geske talks to students, she does not gloss over anything because they need to know the truth about what meth can do. Many people agree that giving teens a glimpse into the ugliness of meth abuse and addiction is the best way to scare them out of ever trying it in the first place. This was the thinking behind the Meth Project, a prevention campaign that was the brainchild of billionaire entrepreneur Tom Siebel. After becoming aware that the meth problem in his home state of Montana had reached epidemic proportions, Siebel wanted to do something. "It's palpable, visible, and very tragic,"[66] he says.

Siebel invested millions of dollars of his own money and in 2005 launched the Meth Project, which has since been cited by the White House as one of the most effective prevention programs. The Meth Project campaign features billboards, radio ads, television spots, newspaper ads, and

> " The Meth Project campaign features billboards, radio ads, television spots, newspaper ads, and online ads, each of which depicts vivid portrayals of the horrors of meth addiction. "

online ads, each of which depicts vivid portrayals of the horrors of meth addiction. The spots were intentionally created to evoke disgust and fear in teens so they will avoid meth altogether, and this is apparent in the program slogan "Not Even Once." Spots show scenarios such as a teenage boy strung out on meth attacking his mother, a young man offering to sell his girlfriend for drugs, and the horrid transformation of a pretty teenage girl into one whose teeth are rotted and whose skin is covered in open sores. Says Siebel: "We're really focused on realism. That's exactly the way addicts look."[67]

Since the Meth Project was launched it has run 269,000 television ads, 300,900 radio spots, and 10,800 billboard ads as well as tens of thousands of print ads. The campaign has expanded from Montana into Arizona, Idaho, Colorado, Wyoming, Georgia, Illinois, and Hawaii. Statistics clearly show that the program has made a positive difference. For example, according to the Arizona Criminal Justice Commission, lifetime meth use by teens in the state has declined by over 65 percent since 2007. Also in Arizona, teen meth use in the past thirty days has declined by nearly 70 percent. Other studies have shown that the Meth Project has been successful in Idaho. Teen meth use dropped 52 percent between 2007 and 2009, and 65 percent of teens surveyed say that they see significant risk in taking meth just once or twice.

> Because meth is such a powerful, addictive drug, and overcoming addiction is so difficult, people often assume that habitual abusers cannot change.

Lives Worth Saving

One of the motivating factors for Siebel's initial creation of the Meth Project was the massive number of people who were being sent to prison for meth-related offenses. In 2005, for instance, Siebel learned that more than half the children in Montana's foster care system and over half the state prisoners were there because of methamphetamine. This was costing the state of Montana about $60 million per year. "Here we consider ourselves the land of the brave and home of the free, or whatever it is," says Siebel, "and we have this great independent, free society, and yet we have the largest rate of incarceration of any society on earth. Most of this is about the War on Drugs. I mean, this is just crazy. You can't put everybody in jail."[68]

Tesja Erickson's life was transformed because somebody believed she was worth saving. A doctor's daughter who was often called an all-American girl as a teen, Erickson first used meth when she was twenty years old—and was immediately hooked. "All it took was once," she says. She spiraled downward from there, reaching the point where she was not only using meth but also dealing it, and she could see no way out. "By the end, I was doing it just to feel normal, just to function," says Erickson. "I wasn't even getting high anymore. The fun ends very quickly, if there ever is any fun to begin with."[69]

Erickson turned her life around because a probation officer cared enough to guide her in a better direction. Today she volunteers with the Idaho Meth Project in the hope that she can help influence teens to not travel the same road she did. She talks to kids in middle school and high school about the dangers of meth because she believes so strongly in the cause—yet she does this at a personal cost because talking about her life as a meth addict is extremely tough. "It's a very traumatic experience to get up in front of people," says Erickson. "It takes a lot out of me, but I need to educate the people of Idaho. There's no reason for people to remain in the dark anymore."[70]

Life After Meth

Because meth is such a powerful, addictive drug, and overcoming addiction is so difficult, people often assume that habitual abusers cannot change. They are wrong, however, and survivors want that to be known. To help raise awareness that people can and do recover from meth addiction, the group Partnership at DrugFree.org (formerly Partnership for a Drug-Free America) and the Office of National Drug Control Policy launched a program called Life After Meth. It features short video spots and documentaries of real people who have suffered because of meth addiction, but who were able to get their lives back.

One documentary is about Steven Reidhead, who is living proof that there is "life after meth"—but before he got to that point, he came face to face with death. His battle with methamphetamine started when he was a teenager and tried it for the first time. Like so many others, he was immediately hooked on the drug and could not get enough of it. He stole money from his family and from his friends, cast aside his plans for college, and stopped caring about anything but getting high. The turning point happened in 2003 when Reidhead was in what he calls a "fleabag" motel room with several other people, including his drug dealer. The dealer became paranoid and attacked Reidhead, stabbing him in the abdomen. He was rushed to the hospital and had to be resuscitated several times, and the EMTs were shocked when he opened his eyes. Referring to one of them, Reidhead says: "He told me that this will all be a waste if you don't get your life in order."[71]

> **Addiction specialists agree that it is hard for habitual abusers to give up methamphetamine, which is why the focus is so heavily on prevention—potential users must be dissuaded from ever trying the drug.**

That was what it took for Reidhead to clean up his life. He began making major changes, including no longer associating with the people who had contributed to his self-destruction. "You gotta change everything about you," says Reidhead. "It wasn't just stop using, it was stop visiting, stop associating, stop loitering—when I decided I was going to get clean I had to change everything. Any old behavior can and will trigger your addiction."[72] He says that his recovery truly began with Narcotics Anonymous. He attended meetings every day, regularly met with his probation officer, and eventually got his life back on track.

Today Reidhead is happily married, the father of two little girls, and the coach of a high school's junior varsity baseball team. He does not hesitate to tell the boys he coaches about his past in the hope that they will learn from it. And even today, he remains vigilant. "Every morning when I wake up I say, what does it take to stay clean today? And then I do it." At the end of his video Reidhead talks directly to those who are listening to his message: "I don't think I could find a better example to let you know that recovery is definitely possible."[73]

Multifaceted Treatment

Addiction specialists agree that it is hard for habitual abusers to give up methamphetamine, which is why the focus is so heavily on prevention—potential users must be dissuaded from ever trying the drug. Treatment can help people recover, however. According to Keith Heinzerling, a physician who specializes in addiction medicine, the most common treatment for meth addiction is behavioral therapy, and several types have been shown to be effective. The first is cognitive behavioral therapy (CBT), which aims to help patients change the way they think about things. In CBT sessions they also learn skills needed to resist their triggers to use drugs. The other type of therapy is contingency management (CM), whereby patients receive immediate reinforcement for positive behavior. Heinzerling explains: "If they provide a urine sample that is negative for methamphetamine they get a reward (often a gift card)."[74]

According to Heinzerling, both types of behavioral therapy can help methamphetamine addicts, "but they are not close to 100% effective." He goes on to say that in his own studies, he and his colleagues found that about one-third of meth addicts were able to remain abstinent from methamphetamine after twelve weeks of treatment. For the most severely addicted meth abusers (those who used the drug daily or almost daily), the success rate with behavioral therapy was only about 5 to 10 percent. "It is clear," Heinzerling explains, "that we need something additional to boost the success rates."[75] The "something,"

> **For so many reasons, methamphetamine is a terrible drug—one that many addicts wish they had never even heard of.**

he says, is likely a medication that would work in tandem with behavioral therapy. Although no medications are currently approved to treat meth addiction, studies to find one (or more than one) are underway by a number of researchers, including Heinzerling's group.

One study that was published in July 2012 resulted in a promising finding about drug therapy for methamphetamine addiction. A team of researchers led by Bankole A. Johnson of the University of Virginia School of Medicine examined the effectiveness of an anticonvulsant drug called topiramate. The drug works by decreasing abnormal excitement in the brain and is usually prescribed to treat epilepsy. But it has also been shown to be effective for some people with alcohol dependence and cocaine addiction.

Johnson's study, conducted at eight sites around the United States, involved evaluating 140 meth addicts to determine the effectiveness of topiramate in treating their addiction. Participants were given either topiramate or a placebo (sugar pill). The team found that while topiramate did not cure meth addiction, it could reduce the amount of meth that addicts take and also reduce relapse rates in those who have quit using meth. "Once a person stops, even for a few days," says Johnson, "topiramate significantly increases their chances for not relapsing. That's very important, because relapse prevention is an important component of addiction medicine." Johnson goes on to say that developing medicines to treat meth addiction is a high priority for researchers. "We've had a lot of success with alcohol treatments, less so with stimulants. So this methamphetamine study is the first time we're beginning to find drugs that actually help."[76]

A Daunting Challenge

For so many reasons, methamphetamine is a terrible drug—one that many addicts wish they had never even heard of. Because meth addiction is difficult to treat and the relapse rate is so high, antidrug groups put most of their focus on prevention programs that will dissuade people from using meth the first time. Although treatment can and does help meth abusers recover, they will save themselves a great deal of misery and health problems if they avoid meth altogether.

How Effective Are Prevention and Treatment Efforts?

❝Methamphetamine addiction can be successfully treated.❞

—National Institute on Drug Abuse (NIDA), "Declines in Methamphetamine Abuse by Youth," *Topics in Brief*, November 2011. www.drugabuse.gov.

An agency of the National Institutes of Health, NIDA seeks to end drug abuse and addiction in the United States.

❝There is little empirical data identifying a specific treatment program as the most effective when it comes to treating meth addiction.❞

—Tennessee District Attorneys General Conference, "Life After Meth," 2011. www.methfreetn.org.

The Tennessee District Attorneys General Conference is charged with overseeing the prompt and efficient administration of justice in Tennessee courts.

* Editor's Note: While the definition of a primary source can be narrowly or broadly defined, for the purposes of Compact Research, a primary source consists of: 1) results of original research presented by an organization or researcher; 2) eyewitness accounts of events, personal experience, or work experience; 3) first-person editorials offering pundits' opinions; 4) government officials presenting political plans and/or policies; 5) representatives of organizations presenting testimony or policy.

"Methamphetamine addicts very often develop severe paranoia and psychosis that does not respond to usual treatments, and can become unstable, irritable and aggressive."

—Narconon International, "Methamphetamine Abuse," 2012. www.narconon.org.

Narconon International helps people who are addicted to drugs by providing educational information and rehabilitation programs.

"Sending addicts to prison is like painting your house when it is on fire; it does not solve the problem."

—Marshall Fisher, "The Status of Methamphetamine: Mississippi's Experience Making Pseudoephedrine Prescription Only," testimony before the US House of Representatives Committee on Government Reform and Oversight, July 24, 2012. http://oversight.house.gov.

Fisher is executive director of the Mississippi Bureau of Narcotics.

"The methamphetamine epidemic does not appear to be slowing, and states must be poised to make critical decisions regarding prevention, education, enforcement, treatment and rehabilitation."

—Jeremy L. Williams, "The Resurgence of Crystal Meth: Trends and State Responses," Council of State Governments *Book of the States*, 2011. http://knowledgecenter.csg.org.

Williams is a policy analyst at the Council of State Governments in Atlanta, Georgia.

"The vast majority of meth addicts . . . will take their psychosis to the grave; they will never get help and clean up, and this is a simple, very sad, fact."

—Jerome Viveiros, "On Amphetamine Psychosis; How It Feels to Have Voices in Your Head," *A Recovered Meth Addict's Blog*, July 29, 2010. http://recoveredmethaddict.wordpress.com.

Viveiros is a recovered methamphetamine addict from Cape Town, South Africa.

❝Improved treatment approaches are needed to produce long-term reductions in methamphetamine use.❞

—Rebecca McKetin et al., "Evaluating the Impact of Community-Based Treatment Options on Methamphetamine Use: Findings from the Methamphetamine Treatment Evaluation Study (MATES)," *Addiction*, July 12, 2012. http://onlinelibrary.wiley.com.

McKetin is a fellow with the Centre for Research on Ageing, Health and Wellbeing at the Australian National University in Canberra, Australia.

❝Since its inception in Wyoming, the Meth Project's prevention program has demonstrated significant results in changing teen attitudes about Meth.❞

—Wyoming Meth Project, "Results," 2012. http://wyoming.methproject.org.

The Wyoming Meth Project is a prevention program aimed at reducing methamphetamine use through public service messaging, public policy, and community outreach.

❝The sad fact is that drug dealers and users will always try to find a way to get their hands on illegal drugs. But there is a common-sense solution that can help stop lawbreakers at the counter, provide law enforcement with critical information, and still allow workers and families access to the medicines they need to remain active and productive.❞

—George Runner, "George Runner on How to Stop Meth in California," *Los Angeles Daily News*, May 22, 2012. www.dailynews.com.

Runner is a member of the California Board of Equalization and a former state senator.

Facts and Illustrations

How Effective Are Prevention and Treatment Efforts?

- A study published in 2012 by a team of researchers from Australia found that most methamphetamine addicts **relapse** within three years of seeking treatment.

- Since the Meth Project prevention program was launched in Montana in 2005, teen methamphetamine use has decreased **63 percent** and meth-related crime has declined **62 percent**.

- According to Michael's House drug treatment facility, studies have shown that in about **80 percent** of crystal meth addicts, relapse occurs between seven and ten months after the completion of treatment.

- The Foundation for a Drug Free World states that **93 percent** of meth abusers in traditional treatment programs return to abusing methamphetamine.

- Internal medicine physician Keith Heinzerling says that no medications are currently approved to treat **methamphetamine addiction**, and the mainstay of treatment is **behavioral therapy**.

- A study published in the July 2011 issue of the medical journal *Molecular Psychiatry* found that among methamphetamine addicts being treated, those whose **brain dopamine function** was the most affected by meth abuse had the highest rate of relapse.

Anti-Meth Program a Success in Wyoming

In 2008 a federal report ranked Wyoming second in the United States for methamphetamine abuse among teenagers. This prompted state health officials to implement the Meth Project, a prevention-oriented campaign that features graphic depictions of the harm meth can do to someone's body. To measure the program's effect on teen awareness of the dangers of the drug, as well as teen attitudes toward meth abuse, a statewide survey of teens was conducted in October 2011. As this graph shows, the campaign is making a difference.

Respondents who said there was a "great risk" of each of the following happening to someone who tries methamphetamine once

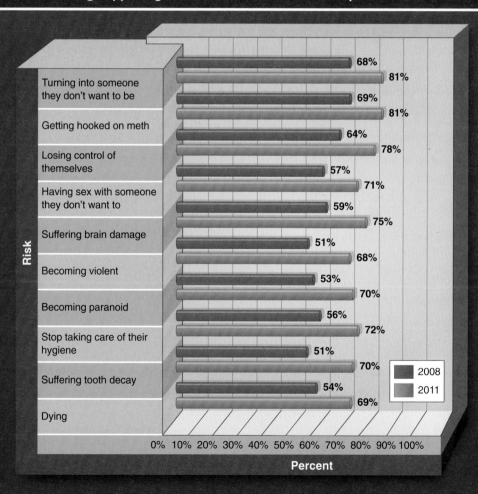

Source: Wyoming Meth Project/Roper, "Wyoming Meth: Use & Attitudes Survey 2011," October 17, 2011. http://foundation.methproject.org.

Treating Meth Addiction

Mental health professionals and addiction experts say that methamphetamine addiction is extremely difficult to treat. One approach that is sanctioned by the National Institute on Drug Abuse and the Substance Abuse and Mental Health Services Administration is known as the Matrix Model, which is detailed in this diagram.

Matrix Model of Methamphetamine Addiction Treatment

Technique	Description/Expectations
Motivational Interviewing	A non-confrontational therapy that focuses on client respect and help in moving forward in treatment, as well as in life. The therapist and patient form a positive relationship and foster success.
12-step Facilitation	Including 12-step programs like Narcotics Anonymous provides a backbone of long-term support.
Family Involvement	Family and friends are encouraged to participate.
Education	Because the Matrix Model is a scientific approach to methamphetamine treatment, the model also educates about drugs, addiction, and the latest addiction research in easy-to-understand ways.
Contingency Management	Positive behaviors are reinforced throughout treatment, and plans are made in advance for the possibility of relapse.
Continuing Care	Meth addicts who stay connected to the methamphetamine treatment environment have better long-term outcomes.

Source: Natasha Tracy (reviewed by Harry Croft, MD), "Treatment for Meth Addiction: Matrix Model of Meth Treatment," Healthy Place, January 18, 2012. www.healthyplace.com.

- According to health officials in Oklahoma, **treatment slots** for meth-amphetamine addiction are in such short supply in the state that people on a waiting list for treatment often end up **addicted, in jail, or dead** before they can be helped.

Lack of Health Insurance Most Common Barrier to Treatment

For a variety of reasons, most people who are addicted to methamphetamine and other illicit drugs do not seek treatment. According to a September 2012 survey by the Substance Abuse and Mental Health Services Administration, the top reason for this was the substance abusers had no health coverage, followed by their reluctance to stop using.

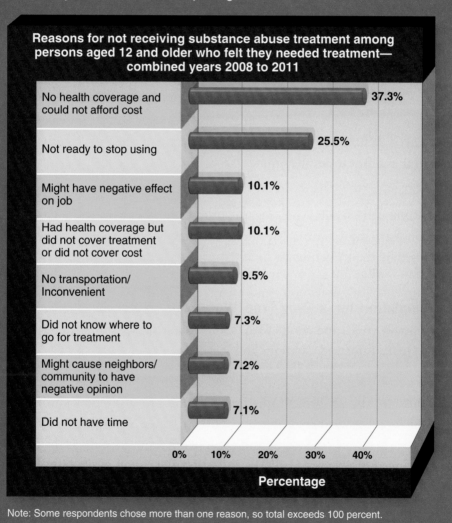

Reasons for not receiving substance abuse treatment among persons aged 12 and older who felt they needed treatment—combined years 2008 to 2011

Reason	Percentage
No health coverage and could not afford cost	37.3%
Not ready to stop using	25.5%
Might have negative effect on job	10.1%
Had health coverage but did not cover treatment or did not cover cost	10.1%
No transportation/Inconvenient	9.5%
Did not know where to go for treatment	7.3%
Might cause neighbors/community to have negative opinion	7.2%
Did not have time	7.1%

Percentage

Note: Some respondents chose more than one reason, so total exceeds 100 percent.

Source: Substance Abuse and Mental Health Services Administration (SAMHSA), "Results from the 2011 National Survey on Drug Use and Health Summary of National Findings," September 2012. www.samhsa.gov.

Key People and Advocacy Groups

Jesús, Adan, and Luis Amezcua: Mexican brothers who founded the notorious Colima Cartel, a methamphetamine production and trafficking operation. After their 1998 arrest and years of legal wrangling, all three were given lengthy prison sentences by Mexican authorities in 2005.

Rob Bovett: The district attorney for Lincoln County, Oregon, the primary author of the state's anti-meth legislation, and a noted authority on methamphetamine.

Lazăr Edeleanu: A Romanian chemist who in 1887 was the first person to synthesize amphetamine.

Dianne Feinstein: A US senator from California who created and co-sponsored the Combat Methamphetamine Epidemic Act, which was passed by the US Congress in 2005.

Foundation for a Drug-Free World: An organization that seeks to empower youth and adults with factual information about drugs so they can make informed decisions and live drug free.

Gene Haislip: A former Drug Enforcement Administration administrator who recognized the dangerous potential of methamphetamine's precursor chemicals (ephedrine and pseudoephedrine) as early as the 1980s and urged government officials to restrict the drugs' availability before the meth problem got out of hand.

Nagayoshi Nagai: A Japanese chemist who in 1885 was the first person to extract ephedrine from the ephedra vulgaris plant.

National Institute on Drug Abuse: An agency of the National Institutes of Health, NIDA seeks to end drug abuse and addiction in the United States.

Office of National Drug Control Policy: A component of the Executive Office of the President, this agency is responsible for directing the federal government's antidrug programs.

Akira Ogata: A Japanese chemist who produced the first crystallized form of methamphetamine in 1919.

Richard Rawson: A neuropsychiatrist who has studied methamphetamine abuse for over two decades, and who created an effective meth addiction treatment called the Matrix Model.

Thomas Siebel: The founder of the Meth Project, a public awareness campaign that began in Montana and uses graphic images and stories to discourage people from ever trying methamphetamine.

US Drug Enforcement Administration: The agency that is responsible for domestic enforcement of federal drug laws, as well as for coordinating and pursuing US drug investigations abroad.

Nora Volkow: The director of the National Institute on Drug Abuse (NIDA) who has extensively researched methamphetamine and its effects on the brain and has made meth abuse a priority during her tenure with the NIDA.

Chronology

1885
Japanese pharmacologist Nagayoshi Nagai is the first to identify and extract ephedrine from the ephedra shrub.

1893
Japanese chemist Nagayoshi Nagai creates a variant of amphetamine that later comes to be known as methamphetamine.

1938
Congress passes the Federal Food, Drug, and Cosmetic Act and establishes the Food and Drug Administration (FDA) to enforce the law.

1940s
To boost energy and fight fatigue, US and British military personnel are given Benzedrine tablets during World War II; methamphetamine is furnished to German and Japanese military personnel.

1976
The FDA approves pseudoephedrine for over-the-counter sale as a decongestant.

1900

1940

1980

1919
Japanese chemist Akira Ogata synthesizes a crystallized version of methamphetamine.

1933
The pharmaceutical firm Smith, Kline and French introduces an amphetamine inhaler, under the brand name Benzedrine, that is sold as an over-the-counter treatment for nasal congestion.

1970
Congress passes the Comprehensive Drug Abuse Prevention and Control Act, which establishes five "schedules" for the classification and control of drug substances that are subject to abuse.

1887
Working in a laboratory at the University of Berlin, Romanian chemist Lazăr Edeleanu becomes the first person to synthesize amphetamine.

1971
The FDA classifies amphetamines and methamphetamine as Schedule II drugs, meaning they are recognized as having therapeutic value but also have a high potential for abuse and addiction.

1988
The US Congress passes the Chemical Diversion and Trafficking Act, which regulates bulk ephedrine and pseudoephedrine and mandates record keeping, reporting, and import/export notifications; the law does not apply to tablets or capsules that contain ephedrine or pseudoephedrine.

2013
A study by Australian researchers finds that methamphetamine users are five times more likely to develop psychosis than people who do not use the drug.

2006
Oregon becomes the first US state to make all drugs (including cold medicines) containing pseudoephedrine available only through a doctor's prescription.

2004
Oklahoma becomes the first state to pass legislation requiring that pseudoephedrine products be placed behind the pharmacy counter, that all sales of the medications be logged, and that in order to buy them customers must show photo identification.

1990

2000

2012
In an effort to dissuade young people from trying methamphetamine, the group Rehabs.com launches a national campaign called *The Horrors of Methamphetamines*, which features graphic, disturbing before and after photographs of people who have abused meth.

1996
President Bill Clinton signs the Comprehensive Methamphetamine Control Act, which strengthens the Drug Enforcement Administration's ability to control precursor chemicals and equipment used to produce methamphetamine.

2005
The US Congress passes the Combat Methamphetamine Epidemic Act. The law aims to curb meth production by requiring retailers to place products containing ephedrine and pseudoephedrine where customers do not have direct access to them, such as behind the counter.

2010
President Barack Obama signs into law the Combat Methamphetamine Enhancement Act, which requires all retail sellers of precursor products such as pseudoephedrine to verify that they train their staff and comply with requirements of the Combat Methamphetamine Epidemic Act.

2011
A report by the United Nations Office on Drugs and Crime ranks amphetamine-type stimulants (such as methamphetamine) as the world's second most widely used drug type after cannabis.

Related Organizations

Crystal Meth Anonymous

4470 W. Sunset Blvd., Suite 107
PMB 555
Los Angeles, CA 90027-6302
phone: (213) 488-4455
website: www.crystalmeth.org

Crystal Meth Anonymous is composed of people for whom drugs, specifically crystal meth, have become a problem, and the only requirement for membership is a desire to stop using. Its website offers information about the twelve-step program and a variety of meth-related publications.

Drug Policy Alliance

131 West 33rd St., 15th Floor
New York, NY 10001
phone: (212) 613-8020 • fax: (212) 613-8021
e-mail: nyc@drugpolicy.org • website: www.drugpolicy.org

The Drug Policy Alliance promotes alternatives to current drug policy that are grounded in science, compassion, health, and human rights. Its website features drug facts, statistics, information about drug laws and individual rights, and a search engine that produces numerous articles about methamphetamine.

Foundation for a Drug-Free World

1626 N. Wilcox Ave., Suite 1297
Los Angeles, CA 90028
phone: (818) 952-5260; toll-free: (888) 668-6378
e-mail: info@drugfreeworld.org • website: www.drugfreeworld.org

The Foundation for a Drug-Free World exists to empower youth and adults with factual information about drugs so they can make informed decisions and live drug free. A wealth of information is available on its website, including a "History of Methamphetamine" section that offers numerous publications about meth.

Meth Project Foundation

PO Box 5287
Redwood City, CA 94063
phone: (650) 299-5270
e-mail: info@methproject.org
website: http://foundation.methproject.org

The Meth Project Foundation is a large-scale prevention program that aims to reduce methamphetamine use through public service messaging, public policy, and community outreach. Its website offers news releases, fact sheets, the *Meth Project* newsletter, reports, and a link to the "Ask Meth Project," which provides even more information about meth.

Michael's House

430 S. Cahuilla Rd.
Palm Springs, CA 92262
phone: (877) 345-8494
website: www.michaelshouse.com

Michael's House is a rehabilitation and treatment center for people suffering from alcohol or drug addiction. Its website's search engine produces a number of articles about methamphetamine abuse and addiction, as does the *Crystal Meth Addiction* blog.

Narconon International

4652 Hollywood Blvd.
Los Angeles, CA 90027
phone: (323) 962-2404 • fax: (323) 962-6872
e-mail: info@narconon.org • website: www.narconon.org

Founded in 1965 by a man who was incarcerated at Arizona State Prison, Narconon International helps people who are addicted to drugs by providing educational information and rehabilitation programs. The "Drug Information" section of its website offers many informative articles about methamphetamine abuse and addiction.

National Institute on Drug Abuse (NIDA)

National Institutes of Health
6001 Executive Blvd., Room 5213
Bethesda, MD 20892-9561
phone: (301) 443-1124
e-mail: information@nida.nih.gov • website: www.drugabuse.gov

The NIDA supports research efforts and ensures the rapid dissemination of research to improve drug abuse prevention, treatment, and policy. The website links to a separate "NIDA for Teens" site, which is designed especially for teenagers and provides a wealth of information about drugs, including methamphetamine.

Office of National Drug Control Policy

750 Seventeenth St. NW
Washington, DC 20503
phone: (800) 666-3332 • fax: (202) 395-6708
e-mail: ondcp@ncjrs.org • website: www.whitehouse.gov

A component of the Executive Office of the President, the Office of National Drug Control Policy is responsible for directing the federal government's antidrug programs. A wide variety of publications about methamphetamine are available through the site's search engine.

Partnership at Drugfree.org

(formerly Partnership for a Drug-Free America)

352 Park Ave. South, 9th Floor
New York, NY 10010
phone: (212) 922-1560 • fax: (212) 922-1570
website: www.drugfree.org

The Partnership at Drugfree.org is dedicated to helping parents and families solve the problem of teenage substance abuse. Its website offers a large number of informative publications that can be accessed through the search engine.

US Drug Enforcement Administration (DEA)

2401 Jefferson Davis Hwy.
Alexandria, VA 22301
phone: (202) 307-1000; toll-free: (800) 332-4288
website: www.justice.gov

The DEA is the United States' top federal drug law enforcement agency. Its website links to a separate site called "Just Think Twice" that is designed for teenagers and features fact sheets, personal experiences, and numerous publications specifically about methamphetamine.

UCLA Integrated Substance Abuse Programs (ISAP)

11075 Santa Monica Blvd., Suite 100
Los Angeles, CA 90025
phone: (800) 310-7700
e-mail: isap@ucla.edu • website: www.uclaisap.org

The ISAP is devoted to research, clinical training, and the coordination of treatment for substance use disorders. A wealth of information about methamphetamine can be found on its MethInformation site, located at www.methinformation.org.

For Further Research

Books
Scott Thomas Anderson, *Shadow People: How Meth-Driven Crime Is Eating at the Heart of Rural America*. Folsom, CA: Coalition for Investigative Journalism, 2012.

Wayne Huffman, *Meth: A Memoir*. Berryville, AR: Midnight Express, 2012.

Lara Norquest, *The Truth About Methamphetamine and Crystal Meth*. New York: Rosen, 2012.

David Parnell and Amy Hammond Hagberg, *Facing the Dragon: How a Desperate Act Pulled One Addict Out of Methamphetamine Hell*. Deerfield Beach, FL: Health Communications, 2010.

Nic Sheff, *We All Fall Down: Living with Addiction*. New York: Hachette, 2011.

Lori L. Stephens, *Trapped: Memoirs of an Ex-Meth Addict and Her Recovery Out of the Insanity of It All*. Bloomington, IN: AuthorHouse, 2011.

US Department of Justice, *Drug Prevention 4 Teens*. Charleston, SC: CreateSpace, 2012.

Kimberly Wollenburg, *Crystal Clean: A Mother's Struggle with Meth Addiction and Recovery*. Charleston, SC: CreateSpace, 2012.

Periodicals
Jon Bardin, "Study Finds Link Between Pseudoephedrine Sales, Meth Busts," *Los Angeles Times*, October 16, 2012.

Ana Campoy, "Micro Meth Labs Run Riot," *Wall Street Journal*, November 2, 2011.

Economist, "Methed Up: The Methamphetamine Business," March 24, 2012.

Abby Goodnough, "States Battling Meth Makers Look to Limit Ingredients," *New York Times*, March 28, 2011.

Joshua Kors, "Crossing the Line," *Current Science*, October 1, 2010.

Nicholas D. Kristof, "Cheap Meth! Cheap Guns! Click Here," *New York Times*, January 2, 2013.

Nick Krug, "Losing the Meth War," *Lawrence* (Kansas) *Journal-World*, March 4, 2012.

Megan McArdle, "Do We Need Even Tighter Controls on Sudafed?" *Atlantic*, February 6, 2012.

Jim Salter, "Mexican Cartels Flood U.S. with Cheap Meth," *Washington Times*, October 11, 2011.

Kirsten Weir, "Drug War: Illegal Drugs Contribute to Crime and Violence Around the World and Around the Corner," *Current Health Teens*, February 2011.

Internet Sources

Brian Doherty, "Meth Myths," *Reason Hit & Run*, blog, April 11, 2011. http://reason.com/blog/2011/04/11/meth-myths.

National Institute on Drug Abuse, *Mind Over Matter*. http://teens.drug abuse.gov/sites/default/files/methamphetamine.pdf.

Oprah, "How Fergie Overcame Her Crystal Meth Addiction," October 21, 2012. www.oprah.com/own-oprahs-next-chapter/How-Fergie -Overcame-Her-Crystal-Meth-Addiction-Video.

Rehabs.com, "The Horrors of Methamphetamines," infographic, 2012. www.rehabs.com/explore/meth-before-and-after-drugs/infographic .html#.US-n6EqS_Y8.

Jim Salter, "Methamphetamine Accidents Fill U.S. Hospitals with Uninsured Patients, Strain Burn Units," *Huffington Post*, January 23, 2012. www.huffingtonpost.com/2012/01/23/methamphetamine-bu rns_n_1222925.html.

Nic Sheff, "My Life as a Teenage Meth Head," *The Fix*, January 27, 2012. www.thefix.com/content/i-was-a-teenage-meth-head-nic-sheff-100 10?page=all.

Lindsey Tanner, "Meth Babies Have Higher Risk for Behavior Problems, Study Finds," *Huffington Post*, March 19, 2012. www.huff ingtonpost.com/2012/03/19/meth-babies-behavior-problems-study _n_1361229.html.

Source Notes

Overview

1. Nic Sheff, "My Life as a Teenage Meth Head," The Fix, January 27, 2012. www.thefix.com.
2. Sheff, "My Life as a Teenage Meth Head."
3. National Institute on Drug Abuse, "What Is Methamphetamine?" September 2006. www.drugabuse.gov.
4. Koichi, "Japan, Land of the Rising Meth," Togufu, April 10, 2012. www.tofugu.com.
5. Rob Bovett, e-mail interview by author, February 24, 2013.
6. Quoted in Mark Schwerin, "WMU Student, Flight Nurse, Joins Fight Against Meth," *WMU News*, Western Michigan University, March 30, 2011. www.wmich.edu.
7. Foundation for a Drug-Free World, "The Truth About Crystal Meth," 2008. www.drugfreeworld.org/sites/default/files/truth-about-crystalmeth-booklet-en.pdf.
8. Crystal, "Crystal's Crash," video, Foundation for a Drug-Free World. www.methproject.org.
9. Foundation for a Drug-Free World, "The Truth About Crystal Meth."
10. Robert Weiss, "Crystal Methamphetamine: The Other Sexual Addiction," *PsychCentral*, blog, September 6, 2012. http://blogs.psychcentral.com.
11. Life or Meth, "Crash 'N' Burn." www.lifeormeth.com.
12. Quoted in Don Wade, "Meth Lab Reports Up 39 Percent Nationally in Past Three Years," *Naples News*, November 18, 2012. www.naplesnews.com.
13. Robert Lucier, participant in PBS *Frontline*, "The Meth Epidemic," May 17, 2011. www.pbs.org.
14. R. Gil Kerlikowske, testimony before the US House of Representatives Committee on Government Reform and Oversight, *Meth Revisited: Review of State and Federal Efforts to Solve the Domestic Methamphetamine Production Resurgence*, July 24, 2012. www.whitehouse.gov.
15. Quoted in Shaun Hittle, "Losing the Meth War," *Lawrence Journal-World*, March 4, 2012. www2.ljworld.com.
16. Weiss, "Crystal Methamphetamine: The Other Sexual Addiction."
17. Tennessee District Attorneys General Conference, "Life After Meth," 2011. www.methfreetn.org.
18. Tennessee District Attorneys General Conference, "Life After Meth."
19. Quoted in Christina Lords, "Breaking Bad Meth Habits in Idaho," *Idaho Statesman*, August 28, 2012. www.idahostatesman.com.

How Serious a Problem Is Methamphetamine Abuse?

20. Quoted in Joshua Rhett Miller, "Meth Rehab: Former Labs a Nightmare for Unwitting Homebuyers," Fox News, June 27, 2012. www.foxnews.com.
21. Quoted in Miller, "Meth Rehab."
22. Kerlikowske, testimony.
23. Kerlikowske, testimony.
24. Quoted in *Akron News Now*, "Akron Mom Found Guilty in Toddler's Death," WAKR, August 27, 2012. www.akronnewsnow.com.

25. Quoted in Justin Juozapavicius, "New Do-It-Yourself Meth Formula Flys Under the Radar of Anti-Drug Laws," *Huffington Post*, August 24, 2009. www.huffingtonpost.com.

26. Quoted in Larry Flowers, "Meth Lab Found on Playground at Murfreesboro School," *WSMV News*, November 6, 2012. www.wsmv.com.

27. Quoted in Rick Iorio, "Meth Lab Fires Continue to Plague Evansville Neighborhoods," *Courier Press*, July 23, 2011. www.courierpress.com.

28. US Department of Justice National Drug Intelligence Center, *National Drug Threat Assessment 2011*, August 2011. www.justice.gov.

29. Jim Salter, "Mexican Drug Cartels Flood U.S. with Cheap Meth," *Washington Times*, October 11, 2012. www.washingtontimes.com.

30. Quoted in Barbara Grijalva, "TPD Says Meth Labs Are Almost Non-Existent in Tucson," *Tucson News Now*, February 26, 2013. www.tucsonnewsnow.com.

31. Quoted in Drug Enforcement Administration, news release, "DEA Announces Results of Operation Knight Stalker," December 17, 2012. www.justice.gov.

32. Quoted in Iorio, "Meth Lab Fires Continue to Plague Evansville Neighborhoods."

What Are the Dangers of Methamphetamine Abuse?

33. Mark Sullivan, "The Real 'Breaking Bad': Confessions of a Former Meth King," *Newsweek Daily Beast*, July 16, 2011. www.thedailybeast.com.

34. Sullivan, "The Real 'Breaking Bad.'"

35. Sullivan, "The Real 'Breaking Bad.'"

36. Sullivan, "The Real 'Breaking Bad.'"

37. Quoted in Tracie Cone and Gosia Wozniacka, "Horrific Murder No Surprise in Meth Capital of US," *Salt Lake Tribune*, January 21, 2012. www.sltrib.com.

38. National Institute on Drug Abuse, "Meth Mouth and Crank Bugs: Meth-a-Morphosis," *Sara Bellum Blog*, January 11, 2010. http://teens.drugabuse.gov.

39. Quoted in Clayton R. Norman, "Addict Keeps Fighting Grasp that Meth Has on Body," *Arizona Daily Star*, July 31, 2011. http://azstarnet.com.

40. Ryan, "Ryan's Story," Meth Project, 2013. www.methproject.org.

41. American Dental Association, "Meth Mouth," *Mouth Healthy*, 2013. www.mouthhealthy.org.

42. Hailey, "Hailey's Story," video, Answers: What Is Meth Mouth? Meth Project, 2013. www.methproject.org.

43. Quoted in Veronique LaCapra, "'Shake-and-Bake' Meth Causes Uptick in Burn Victims," NPR, February 7, 2012. www.npr.org.

44. Quoted in Rosemary Parker, "Taxpayers Burned by Meth, Too: Chemical Mishaps Cost Thousands of Dollars in Medical Bills," MLive, April 3, 2011. www.mlive.com.

45. Dennis Potter, a participant in "'Shake-and-Bake' Meth Causes Uptick in Burn Victims," NPR, February 7, 2012. www.npr.org.

46. Quoted in LaCapra, "'Shake-and-Bake' Meth Causes Uptick in Burn Victims."

47. March of Dimes, "Alcohol and Drugs," January 2008. www.marchofdimes.com.

48. Quoted in Nancy Shute, "Kids Exposed to Meth in Womb Can Struggle with Behavior Problems," NPR, March 19, 2012. www.npr.org.

49. Quoted in Norman, "Addict Keeps Fighting Grasp that Meth Has on Body."

Have Laws Reduced Methamphetamine Production and Use?

50. Quoted in Wayne Greene, "New Laws, More Treatment Both Needed in Drug Fight, Former Users Say," *Tulsa World*, May 18, 2012. www.tulsaworld.com.

51. Rob Bovett, "How to Kill the Meth Monster," *New York Times*, November 16, 2010. www.nytimes.com.
52. Ronald E. Brooks, "Statement for the Record," testimony before the US House of Representatives Committee on Government Reform and Oversight, July 24, 2012. http://oversight.house.gov.
53. Brooks, "Statement for the Record."
54. Joseph T. Rannazzisi, "The Status of Meth: Oregon's Experience Making Pseudoephedrine Prescription Only," statement before the US Senate Caucus on International Narcotics Control, April 13, 2010. www.justice.gov.
55. Marshall Fisher, "The Status of Methamphetamine: Mississippi's Experience Making Pseudoephedrine Prescription Only," testimony before the US House of Representatives Committee on Government Reform and Oversight, July 24, 2012. http://oversight.house.gov.
56. Quoted in Juozapavicius, "New Do-It-Yourself Meth Formula Flys Under the Radar of Anti-Drug Laws."
57. Lucier, "The Meth Epidemic."
58. Government Accountability Office, "Drug Control: State Approaches Taken to Control Access to Key Methamphetamine Ingredient Show Varied Impact on Domestic Drug Labs," January 2013. www.gao.gov.
59. Fisher, "The Status of Methamphetamine."
60. Bovett, "The Meth Epidemic."
61. Jeremy L. Williams, "The Resurgence of Crystal Meth: Trends and State Responses," Council of State Governments *Book of the States*, 2011. http://knowledgecenter.csg.org.
62. Fisher, "The Status of Methamphetamine."
63. Fisher, "The Status of Methamphetamine."

How Effective Are Prevention and Treatment Efforts?

64. Kiyana Geske, "Former Meth Addict Shares Story to Save Others," video, KOAA News, February 6, 2013. www.koaa.com.
65. Geske, "Former Meth Addict Shares Story to Save Others."
66. Quoted in Corey Binns, "The Anti-Drug Lord," Huffpost Healthy Living, June 18, 2008. www.huffingtonpost.com.
67. Quoted in Binns, "The Anti-Drug Lord."
68. Quoted in James Verini, "Meth Mouth: Tom Siebel's Brash Anti-Crystal Campaign," *Fast Company*, May 1, 2009. www.fastcompany.com.
69. Quoted in Lords, "Breaking Bad Methods in Idaho."
70. Quoted in Lords, "Breaking Bad Methods in Idaho."
71. Steven Reidhead, "Steven," video by Nico Sabenorio, *Cultural Weekly*, 2011. www.culturalweekly.com.
72. Reidhead, "Steven."
73. Reidhead, "Steven."
74. Keith Heinzerling, "Why Do We Need a Medication to Treat Methamphetamine Addiction?," UCLASARx, April 1, 2011. www.uclasarx.org.
75. Heinzerling, "Why Do We Need a Medication to Treat Methamphetamine Addiction?"
76. Quoted in Josh Barney, "U. Va. Study: Medication Can Help Recovering Meth Addicts Stay Sober," UVA Today, June 20, 2012. http://news.virginia.edu.

List of Illustrations

Index

Index

About the Author

Peggy J. Parks holds a bachelor of science degree from Aquinas College in Grand Rapids, Michigan, where she graduated magna cum laude. An author who has written more than a hundred educational books for children and young adults, Parks lives in Muskegon, Michigan, a town that she says inspires her writing because of its location on the shores of Lake Michigan.